W9-ABN-262

"Takes a real approach to describe why some retailers prospered and others failed through each wave of retail history. Lewis and Dart's use of case examples brings the book to life, clearly spelling out how customers and the competitive environment have changed and how retailers today must connect with their customers and take control of their value chain to not only be successful, but survive."

—*Ken Hicks, chairman and CEO, Foot Locker, Inc., and former COO of JCPenney*

"*The New Rules of Retail: Competing in the World's Toughest Marketplace* is an important and instructive read for industry veterans and newcomers alike. Lewis and Dart provide a practical roadmap for success in the rapidly evolving environment, along with an assessment of the retailers who 'get it.' With the authors' dire prediction that 50 percent of retailers will be unable to survive the transition to Wave III, this is a must-read for everyone in the business today!"

—*Jane Elfers, president and CEO, The Children's Place*

"This book is an essential read for anyone who is interested in a history of what drives 70 percent of the U.S. economy and the many challenges expected to be faced in the future. Like we are now seeing in politics, the voter/consumer is in the driver's seat, and those serving her had better take heed."

—*Allen Questrom, former CEO, JCPenney, Federated Department Stores, and Barney's*

"*The New Rules of Retail* is a must-read for students of contemporary retailing. Full of meaningful insights about the current environment, the authors chart the course for a successful retail future."

—*Paul Charron, former CEO of Liz Claiborne*

"Lewis and Dart have written an interesting and thoroughly researched book that traces the evolution of the retail business from the distant past to the looming future. Clearly, they know and understand all the players—well worth reading."

—*Marvin Traub, former president and CEO, Bloomingdales*

"*The New Rules of Retail* is an incredibly interesting and a provocative read. I thoroughly enjoyed the authors' insight on past events. I look forward to debate and dialogue about their predictions for the future."

—*Tom Wyatt, president, Old Navy*

"Lewis and Dart give a very accurate view of the past history of retailing. But more importantly, they offer an insightful and strategic view of the consumers and business models needed to support its future."

—*Claudio Del Vecchio, CEO, Brooks Brothers*

"*The New Rules of Retail* shows how to win in an unprecedented environment where consumers have instant access to hundreds of choices for everything they need. Lewis and Dart's recommendations are dramatic, but they show that the consequences for those who stick with the status quo will be dire. A highly original and insightful book."

—*Mark Sarvary, CEO, Tempur-Pedic International Inc.*

"Lewis and Dart have so many thought-provoking ideas that I used up a box of paper clips marking the pages I wanted my various department heads to read. And they're easy to follow—I understood the concept of a 'neurologically connective experience' right away. All future decisions in retailing and wholesaling will be influenced by this book."

—*Bud Konheim, CEO, Nicole Miller*

"Lewis and Dart have shown once again that they have their fingers on the pulse of both consumer needs and the ever-changing retail industry. *The New Rules of Retail* is a must-read for anyone who wants to not only survive but to thrive in the decades to come."

—*Kevin M. Burke, president and CEO,*
American Apparel & Footwear Association

"*The New Rules of Retail* is a powerful analysis of the tectonic shifts that have transformed this industry, and it reveals the secrets of succeeding in today's new economic and digital environment. Authors Robin Lewis and Michael Dart know retailing inside and out and their thought-provoking book, with its incisive perspective, proves it."

—*Tracy Mullin, former president and CEO,*
National Retail Federation

Property of:
◊ **Follett**
Training and Development Department

THE NEW RULES OF RETAIL

COMPETING IN THE WORLD'S TOUGHEST MARKETPLACE

Robin Lewis & Michael Dart

palgrave
macmillan

THE NEW RULES OF RETAIL
Copyright © Robin Lewis and Michael Dart, 2010.
All rights reserved.

First published in 2010 by PALGRAVE MACMILLAN® in the U.S.—a
division of St. Martin's Press LLC, 175 Fifth Avenue, New York, NY
10010.

Where this book is distributed in the UK, Europe and the rest of the
world, this is by Palgrave Macmillan, a division of Macmillan Publishers
Limited, registered in England, company number 785998, of
Houndmills, Basingstoke, Hampshire RG21 6XS.

Palgrave Macmillan is the global academic imprint of the above
companies and has companies and representatives throughout the
world.

Palgrave® and Macmillan® are registered trademarks in the United
States, the United Kingdom, Europe and other countries.

ISBN: 978-0-230-10572-0

Library of Congress Cataloging-in-Publication Data
Lewis, Robin, 1940–
    The new rules of retail : competing in the world's toughest
marketplace / Robin Lewis and Michael Dart
    p.   cm.
    Includes index.
    ISBN 978-0-230-10572-0
    1. Retail trade.   2. Retail trade—Management.   3. Retail trade—
Technological innovations.   4. Wholesale trade.   5. Consumer
satisfaction.   I. Dart, Michael.   II. Title.
    HF5429.L4854   2010
    658.8'7—dc22

                                                                    2010039095

A catalogue record of the book is available from the British Library.

Design by Letra Libre, Inc.

First edition: December 2010

10   9   8   7   6   5   4   3   2   1

Printed in the United States of America.

CONTENTS

PART 3

THE MASTERS

ACKNOWLEDGMENTS

As we began to finalize our thesis, we spent many hours and days pouring over what seemed like tons of research, digging for supportive nuggets and even whole veins to back our logic and strengthen our vision of how the transformation of the industry is going to play out.

In the middle of this yeoman's quest, we realized that between us we had another untapped and enormously rich resource: our past and current professional colleagues; a great number of C-level and senior executives throughout the retail and other consumer-facing industries that we had become friendly with over the years; many academicians; and various industry association leaders.

We sought many of them out and received great insight, much of it profound, and more importantly their positive support and sincere interest in reading our final product.

Others who were not directly involved with our efforts, and many who were simply business colleagues over the years, nevertheless provided knowledge and strategic insights that later became useful in the shaping of our thesis. We want to thank them as well.

At the end of the day, by the time we put pen to paper or fingers to keyboard, we not only knew that our thesis was on track for driving the transformation, but that it was made even more robust through all of our past knowledge sources as well as our direct conversations with the executives whose businesses were in the middle of the fundamental changes taking place.

More importantly, we were honored that these great friends, colleagues and professional associates, both past and present, were interested enough to give of their time to provide us with invaluable perspectives and knowledge.

Angela Ahrendts, CEO, Burberry

David Bell, Operating Adviser, Pegasus Capital Advisors; Senior Adviser, AOL Inc.

Phil Black, former Publisher, *Apparel Strategist;* CNN correspondent

Heather Blonkenfeld, Marketing Director, Kurt Salmon Associates

Paul Blum, CEO Emeritus, David Yurman

Pete Born, Executive Editor, Beauty, *Womens' Wear Daily*

Pauline Brown, Managing Director, Carlyle Group

Kevin Burke, President and CEO, American Apparel and Footwear Association

Tom Burns, Senior Vice President, Doneger Inc.

Vanessa Castagna, former CEO, JCPenney; former Executive Chairwoman, Mervyn's

Lee Chaden, CEO Emeritus, Hanes Brands

Paul Charron, Chairman and CEO Emeritus, Liz Claiborne; Senior Adviser, Warburg Pincus; Managing Partner, Fidus Investment Partners

David Chu, Founder and CEO Emeritus, Nautica

Michael Coady, CEO Emeritus, Fairchild Publications

Arnold Cohen, CEO, Mahoney & Cohen

Bruce Cohen, Partner, Kurt Salmon Associates

Mark Cohen, Professor of Marketing, Columbia University Graduate Business School; former Chairman and CEO, Sears Canada

Kathryn Cordes, Director, Global Marketing and Operations, Deloitte

Bill Crain, former Vice Chairman, VF Corporation

Bill D'Arienzo, Founder and CEO, Wm. D'Arienzo Associates

Claudio Del Vecchio, Chairman and CEO, Retail Brand Alliance; owner of Brooks Brothers

John Donahoe, Director, President and CEO, eBay

Jane Elfers, CEO, The Children's Place Retail Stores

Joe Ellis, author of *Ahead of the Curve;* former Partner, Goldman Sachs

Pamela Ellsworth, Professor, Department of International Trade and Marketing and Chairperson, Global Fashion Management Graduate Program, FIT

Kathy Elsessor, Managing Director and Head of Consumer Retail Group, Goldman Sachs

Ruth Finley, Founder and President, Fashion Calendar

Ben Fischman, CEO and President, Retail Convergence Inc. brand Rue La La

Mike Fitzgerald, former President, Delta Galil; Senior Vice President, Business Development, Delta Galil

Neal Fox, President and CEO, the Cross brand

Don Franceschini, CEO emeritus, former Vice Chairman and CEO, Personal Products; retired, Sara Lee Apparel

Sally Garcia, Administrative Assistant, Kurt Salmon Associates

ACKNOWLEDGMENTS

Marc Gobé, CEO, Emotional Branding LLC, author of *Emotional Branding*

Michael Gould, Chairman and CEO, Bloomingdales

Nick Graham, Founder and former CEO, Joe Boxer

Bob Grayson, Founder, Robert C. Grayson & Associates / The Grayson Company

Rob Gregory, former COO and President, VF Corporation

Joe Gromek, Director, President and CEO, Warnaco

Mindy Grossman, CEO and Director, Home Shopping Network

Gilbert Harrison, Founder, Chairman and CEO, Financo

Clark Hinkley, CEO Emeritus, Talbot's

Brendan Hoffman, CEO, Lord & Taylor

Mary Beth Holland, Founder and owner, Sutton Place Capital Management

Roy Johnson, Instructor, Department of Communication Studies, Baruch College, City University of New York

Ed Jones, Chairman, Jones Texas Inc.

Andy Kahn, Chairman, Kahn Lucas Lancaster, Inc.

Harvey Kanter, President and CEO, MooseJaw

Sonia Kashuk, Founder and owner, Sonia Kashuk beauty brand

Natalie Kennedy, Business Consultant

Renee Klein, Merchandiser, Gilt Groupe

Bud Konheim, Cofounder and CEO, Nicole Miller

William Lauder, Executive Chairman, The Estee Lauder Companies

Margot Lewis, Founder and CEO, Platform Media NY

Claire Liu, Consultant, Kurt Salmon Associates

Walter Loeb, Consultant and Retail Expert

Terry Lundgren, Chairman, President and CEO, Macy's

Dan MacFarlan, former Vice Chairman, VF Corporation

Margaret Mager, former Managing Director and Business Unit Leader—Retail Industry, Goldman Sachs

Arthur Martinez, Chairman and CEO Emeritus, Sears

Mackey McDonald, former Chairman and CEO, VF Corporation

Bob Mettler, former Chairman and CEO, Macy's West

Larry Mondry, former CEO, CSK Auto Corporation

Tracy Mullin, former President and CEO, NRF

Jack Mulqueen, Founder and owner, Mulqueen Sportswear

Karen Murray, President, Nautica brand

Tom Murray, President and CEO, Calvin Klein

Ed Nardoza, Editor-in-Chief, Fairchild Fashion Group

Chuck Nesbit, Executive VP and COO, McMurray Fabrics, Inc

Blake Nordstrom, CEO, Director and President, Nordstrom

D. Scott Olivet, Chairman, Oakley; CEO, RED Digital Camera

Kirk Palmer, CEO, Kirk Palmer & Associates

Cindy Palusamy, Consultant, CP Strategy Inc. Partners & Colleagues, Kurt Salmon Associates

Frank Pickard, Vice President and Treasurer, VF Corporation

John Pomerantz, CEO Emeritus, Leslie Fay

Stefan Preston, former CEO, Bendon Intimates

Allen Questrom, CEO Emeritus, Federated Department Stores, JCPenney and Barney's

Madison Riley, Principal, Kurt Salmon Associates

Bruce Roberts, former President, Textile Distributors Association

Rick Roberts, Cofounder and Partner, Cynthia Steffe Designs

Ellen Rohde, former President, Vanity Fair Intimates

Doug Rossiter, Vice President and Program Director, The

Advantage Group International, Toronto

Judy Russell, Publisher, *Apparel Strategist;* Partner, The Robin Report

Peter Sachse, Chief Marketing Officer, Macy's

Mark Sarvary, CEO and President, Tempur-Pedic

Chris Schaller, former CEO, Forstmann & Co.

Denise Seegal, former President, Liz Claiborne

Mike Setola, President and CEO, MacGregor Golf Co.

Pam Grunder Sheiffer, President, P. Joyce Associates

Jane Singer, Marketing Consultant

Tony Spring, President, Bloomingdale's

Marty Staff, CEO, Joseph Abboud Brand

Cynthia Steffe, Cofounder and Partner, Cynthia Steffe Designs

Michael Steinberg, former CEO, Macy's West; Director, Fossil Inc.

Jeff Streader, former President, Kellwood

Trudy Sullivan, President & CEO, Talbot's

Burt Tansky, former CEO, Neiman Marcus

Jock Thompson, Executive Vice President, Scope Apparel

Olivia Thompson, Marketing Consultant

Miranda Tisdale, Consumer Research Manager, Kohl's

Marvin Traub, retired CEO, Bloomingdale's; President, Marvin Traub Associates

Mike Ullman, Chairman and CEO, JCPenney

Paco Underhill, Founder, CEO and President, Envirosell

Hal Upbin, CEO emeritus, Kellwood

Jeanette Wagner, Consultant and former Vice Chair, Estee Lauder

Kenneth Walker, Managing Director, Republic of Innovation

Dee Warmath, Vice President, Retail Insights, NPD

Manny Weintraub, founder and CEO, Emanuel Weintraub Associates

Bill Williams, retired President and CEO, Harry & David

Eric Wiseman, CEO and President, VF Corporation

Mai Mai Tsai Wythes, Business Consultant

Lastly we would like to give a very special thanks to our agents, Edward Necarsulmer IV and Rebecca Strauss of McIntosh & Otis. Without their belief in the relevancy and timeliness of our thesis, and their dogged, unyielding determination to find a publisher, this book would still be but a dream.

And, of course, the ultimate thanks to Airié Stuart who decided to publish this book, and to the editors and staff at Palgrave Macmillan who actually made it happen.

PROLOGUE

TSUNAMI

In April 2010, Millard "Mickey" Drexler, the CEO of J. Crew, remarked that we were in an era in which we were seeing the "comeback of great retailers."[1] This despite the clear fact that, in the wake of the recent recession, consumer confidence was still low. Drexler was observing the return of those retailers whose business models, strategies and consumer focus were great enough not only to carry them through the recession but also to let them make a quick comeback by reporting growth and market-share gains. On the other side were the strugglers, those retailers and consumer businesses losing market share and facing insolvency. Their failure to rebound was due to poor business models and an inability to respond to rapidly changing consumer demands. So, what did retailers learn from the Great Recession?

The Summit

October 29, 2008, was a wind-whipped, gray day, characteristic of New York City in the fall and fitting for the unprecedented and ur-

gent meeting of twenty-one of the country's leading retail CEOs.
The early morning meeting was convened at New York's Fashion
Institute of Technology. Among the assembled group was co-host
Burt Tansky, CEO of Neiman Marcus, an iconic guru in the world
of luxury and well-known and respected by retailers, designers,
and luxury brand leaders around the world. Joining Burt was a
group of his fellow retail kingpins: Mickey Drexler of J. Crew, and
former CEO of the Gap who led its meteoric growth to become
the world's largest apparel retailer during the 1990s, putting
Drexler on the cover of *Fortune* magazine, following which he took
the "hit" for Gap's collapse; Lew Frankfort of Coach, Inc., who acquired the brand back from Sara Lee, where it had been stagnating
for years, and built it to become one of the most powerful accessories brands in the world; Brendan Hoffman of Lord & Taylor, a
young upstart in the retail world who nevertheless was well on his
way to turning the long-dormant and stale Lord & Taylor brand
back to its previous luster; Claudio Del Vecchio of Brooks Brothers, also a turn-around Messiah, restoring the brand to its position
as the arbiter of men's clothing and sportswear; Mindy Grossman
of Home Shopping Network, Inc; who transformed the brand
from selling a bunch of stuff on TV to inviting viewers into Wolfgang Puck's kitchen where he conducts cooking lessons, as one of
many addictive viewing experiences now provided by HSN;
Michael Weiss of Express, called back out of semi-retirement to
rescue the brand he had once built as one of the first apparel specialty store chains in the United States; Tom Murray of Calvin
Klein, largely responsible for the designer's preeminent and powerful position throughout the world; Joe Gromek of Warnaco, who
took over when the business was about to collapse and managed it
back to profitable growth, including the global expansion of their
Calvin Klein retail business; Matt Rubel of Collective Brands, also
a pioneer in the world of retailing, new to Collective Brands and already adding to its list of brands, including its own private brands,
but also fostering innovation in marketing and accelerating its e-

commerce presence; and Jim Gold of Bergdorf Goodman, a young protégé of Burt Tansky, widely respected for his leadership as well as his keen eye for successful luxury products.

Their purpose was nothing short of understanding and addressing the economic tsunami that was just beginning to wash over the entire world, with projected devastating effects on consumer spending, and therefore the entire retail industry. To describe this as a highly unusual gathering of some of retailing's most powerful and iconic figures—many of them fierce competitors—would be an understatement. However, extraordinary times require extraordinary measures.

And on that same fateful morning in Manhattan, one could find any number of people whose lives were dramatically affected by the enormity of the economic collapse, also reflective of the challenges about to be addressed by the CEO's. The following were three conversations with individuals who requested anonymity.

First, a regional manager for Linens 'N Things had just lost her job. After she'd spent twenty years in retailing, this was a devastating loss. Staring at her company's bankruptcy announcement, she fought back an urge to cry. "I knew that we were not doing things as well as we could, but when we got bought by the big private equity guys I thought I was safe. They would not have bought us if we were doing that badly," she said softly, her voice cracking with emotion. "Could anyone have seen this coming? Why did we have to go? If I work in retail again I want to be in a place that is going to last." Her story was being replayed across the country, as thousands of employees received similar news from bankrupt retailers. Mary put the envelope on the table, made a cup of coffee and worried about how she was going to pay her bills.

Another aggressive, hardworking retail investment manager had made a fortune for her firm over the previous five years. But it all disappeared in a series of what were, in hindsight, disastrous investment decisions. The most prominent involved Circuit City, which during the years leading up to the crash was a

$10–12 billion company. Its depressed share price seemed like an opportunity for someone to buy a large enough stake to force the management team to make the right changes. Susan pursued that strategy, increasing her investment with each market swing and pushing the company to make more and more radical changes. Her only downside risk would have been a private equity takeover with a nice premium to the price she paid. But her bet was against that happening and rather that the company would reestablish itself against its competitor Best Buy. If that happened, the share price would return a substantial multiple.

Neither of those scenarios played out. Circuit City went bankrupt, wiping out everything she had invested. Devastated, she knew this probably meant the end of her career. "The hardest thing I ever faced in my life was the firm's partners, and having to explain to them why I kept going with this. I really need to know for the partners and myself if this disaster could have been avoided. What could I have looked for that would have guided me away from continuing to invest in Circuit City? The reason I lost money was accelerated by the financial crisis, but I missed something that led me to one of the weakest players."

Finally, a typical consumer and avid shopper at the time opened her credit card bill and looked at her new limit. It had dropped from $3500 to $1500. She had never seen this before. In fact, for most of the last few years, her mailbox had been full of cut-rate credit card offers, many of them even offering the ability to defer payments against the principal until she graduated. "I thought I was responsible with my payments, but this was a major shock. I knew at that moment that I was going to cut back on my spending and things were going to change."

When pressed on what would have to change, she talked about cutting back on shopping for nonessentials. Glancing around her cramped apartment, she referred to "meaningless stuff like this." But then she stopped, leaned forward and said with a smile, "But you know the thing I won't stop doing is getting to Zara on the first Tuesday of every month. They have such cool stuff and that's the day all the new things arrive. I'm not going to give up on that!"

As these three women faced their own tsunami-like personal disasters, which portended major changes in their lives as well as the lives of consumers across the nation. The urgent meeting of the CEOs was about to convene in lower Manhattan. This meeting would also mean major disruption and a transformation of the entire retail industry in response to the coming paradigm shift among consumers.

Cohost Burt Tansky strode into the meeting room to join his peers. Tansky had led one of the most successful retail businesses in the industry to extraordinary levels of performance, but the recent crisis had seen his store sales shrink by 30 percent, an unprecedented decline. And this number was well within the range of every other attendee's business, representing the dire condition of the entire industry. Among several of Tansky's comments upon calling the meeting together was a reflection on the fact that in his entire career he had not lived through a downturn as severe, and without some sense of its end, including the four prior recessions. Burt was joined by his cohost, Gilbert Harrison, founder and CEO of Financo Securities LLC, a leading independent investment banking boutique specializing in retail. The meeting opened with an economic overview. The numbers were staggering.

Household debt was 140 percent of income, the highest ever. Mortgage defaults were accelerating, now at 15 percent on prime mortgages. The country had been in a recession for over twelve months. Unemployment was accelerating, projected to pass 10 percent. And the recent interest-rate drops, reaching close to zero, had no noticeable impact on highly negative consumer sentiment. Indeed, the consumer confidence index had reached its lowest point in recorded history.

As the group pondered the impact of these metrics alongside an unprecedented projection of crashing retail sales and a bloodbath of anticipated bankruptcies, you could have heard a pin drop.

In a bit of gallows humor, Burt Tansky quipped: "It reminds me of orientation day in college, when we all gathered in the auditorium to hear the dean's welcome. Remember when he said, 'Look to your right and look to your left—two of you won't be graduating'?"

Mickey Drexler responded: "But that excludes everybody in this room, right, Burt?"[2]

As the group chuckled over this exchange, the irony was palpable; the fear was blooming just beneath the surface that none of them would be exempt from the disastrous downturn they were about to confront.

As they discussed the implications, both short and long term, for their businesses, they unanimously agreed that this was not just another recession in which consumers could be counted on to bounce back to their obsessively consumptive ways. This recession would be historic, possibly touching off a true paradigm shift in consumers' "value orientation" and behavior.

This idea was given further credence by another legendary leader who was not in attendance at FIT. Just a day earlier, Allen Questrom, famed turnaround CEO of several giant retail companies—Federated Department Stores, Barneys, JCPenney and others—spoke at the *Women's Wear Daily* CEO Summit. Among his other remarks, he cautioned that "this will likely be the longest and deepest recession since the depression . . . there will be no quick bounce back . . . maybe five to ten years, and, when we come out of it, we will all have to understand value differently."[3]

Those three words, "understanding value differently," spoke volumes about the new world that would emerge at the end of the economic quagmire, and how consumers' value reorientation would force a corresponding shift across all of retailing—driving the transformation of the retail, wholesale and manufacturing business models.

Although these value shifts probably would have happened eventually, even in a more normal economic environment, the transformation was greatly accelerated by the recession. It forced an abrupt pause to a nearly thirty-year binge on consumption and the relentless pursuit of quantity (more and more stuff, faster and cheaper) and gave further impetus to a consumer trend desiring quality over quantity—special or novel products of superior construction—and the growing desire for great shopping experiences vs. shopping for "stuff" in great big stores.

On a more esoteric level, the economic meltdown had the potential to drive a cultural shift from one of demanding instant gratification to the possibility that we might once again understand the value of earned gratification. Instead of compulsive spending and consumption, in other words, we might begin saving for something better, or investing in growth or greater productivity.

The CEOs discussed the potential issues and scenarios coming out of these shifts. Mickey Drexler, for example, took a shot at Neiman Marcus and Bergdorf Goodman, warning that even the wealthiest of Neiman's loyal customers would no longer pay a thousand dollars for a designer handbag when they believe that it is really worth only seven hundred.

Drexler's point was that price would no longer equal value, and that value would no longer be measured by price. Rather, today's consumers are savvy enough to understand a product's intrinsic quality, the level of workmanship it requires and (generally) what it costs to make. From Bergdorf Goodman down to Wal-Mart, therefore, fair-value pricing will ultimately be in the eye of that most powerful and all-knowing entity, the consumer. Wal-Mart has understood this from its inception in 1962; Drexler was declaring that now the most rarefied luxury purveyors would soon be forced to follow suit.

If Drexler's observation on the paradigm shift in consumers' values needed support, it came just a little over two months later in December, as Wal-Mart CEO Lee Scott gave the keynote address at the opening of the National Retail Federation's massive annual convention. Of consumers' behavior, Scott remarked: "The appetite is toward living a little differently. I wonder whether shopping habits haven't changed. I'm not convinced that consumers are going to have this same immediate desire to go right back to consumption and debt."[4]

His address was covered on the front page of *Women's Wear Daily* the very next day, with the headline: "Shopping Is So Passé: Wal-Mart CEO Foresees New Consumer Mind-Set."[5]

As the FIT meeting drew to a close, then, three things were obvious: The CEOs were headed into a very long and deep economic mess in which it would be difficult to survive, much less thrive; the world as they had known it just a few months ago had fallen apart, and was set to fundamentally change; and, most important, they would be forced to fundamentally change their businesses.

In fact, "fundamentally" would turn out to be an understatement.

INTRODUCTION

THE STORY

The economic tsunami and fateful meeting of industry chiefs provides the perfect symbolic backdrop for our story. However, as we discussed this with many of these CEOs and others, we believed that it merely punctuated the breaking point of a real and larger wave that was building long before the Great Recession.

Having met earlier at an off-site conference of the Carlyle Group's consumer and retail practice, we shared our views and quickly realized that we both believed the consumer and retail industry was going through an epic transformation. From our combined left- and right-brained approaches we decided to explore and explain this transformation as we saw it.

The Authors

We have both been students of, and strategic consultants for, the retail and related consumer products industries, in varied and different professional roles throughout our combined sixty-year careers.

Robin Lewis has over forty years of strategic operating experience and consulting in the retail and related consumer products industries. He has worked for DuPont, VF Corporation, *Women's Wear Daily* (WWD), Goldman Sachs and has consulted for Kohl's department stores. He also writes and publishes *The Robin Report* and is a professor at the Graduate School of Professional Studies at the Fashion Institute of Technology (FIT), teaching the very thesis of this book.

Michael Dart, a senior partner and managing director at Kurt Salmon Associates (KSA), heads up strategy for their private equity practice. Having also spent fourteen years at Bain & Co., where he was a partner, he has over twenty years of consulting experience. During his career he has worked with many of the leaders in the consumer products and retail industries, as well as major private equity firms. These include Microsoft, Michaels Arts & Crafts, Bank One (now J. P. Morgan), Blackstone, TH Lee and the Carlyle Group.

His consulting skills were recognized by *Consulting* magazine, which named him one of the top twenty-five consultants in the United States in 2010.

Our Goal

Our goal is to provide an understanding of the overall pattern of change in the retail and consumer industries over the past few decades: to identify how and why consumers have been changing; how the industry structure is shifting in response to these changes; and, ultimately, which businesses will win and lose. Once these patterns are determined, we can view every retailer and consumer business in that context, and quickly assess their individual trajectories.

For example, what can we learn from the collapse of Circuit City or Linens 'N Things? What were their relationships to the retail industry they competed in? What could they have done to transform themselves for survival? Was their collapse predictable? We discovered, by analyzing them more closely, that they were but one small cog in the enormously dynamic wheel of change over the last century. It wasn't just about Circuit City, ca. 2008—that was merely one of many retail implosions. It was about a greater relevance and connectivity to the entire economy, the retail industry and our entire culture.

To understand the demise of Circuit City, it is not enough to simply understand its strategic, financial, operating and competitive missteps during the late 2000s. This would ignore the deeper and more profound, century-long evolution of retailing, the force of which would have destroyed these retailers regardless of the severe recession. With such a truncated understanding, the leaders of these failed businesses, as well as those across the entire retail spectrum, therefore carry their old notions forward and continue to make the same strategic mistakes.

What about all of retailing, the bigger picture over the last twenty-five years, the opening of more and more stores and the shoving of more and more stuff at the consumer, well before the economic meltdown? How and why was all this happening? How was it changing? What were the consequences?

What about consumers? What drove their compulsive, almost obsessive consumption over all those years? Why the spending frenzy? Did it create happiness and satisfaction? Where are consumers now headed and what are they looking for?

We seek to provide an understanding of these factors and how they evolved over time. We also describe how the recession, ca. 2008, merely accelerated many of the changes that were already occurring. With knowledge of the evolutionary forces, we can project what this new, changed world will look like: its economy, its culture, its retailers and consumers.

The Three Waves of Retailing

Retailing has arrived at this transformative moment after a 150-year evolution, or three waves. Retail strategies and business models were forced to change during each wave in response to a growing economy, shifting consumer priorities and increased competition. Each wave of growth provided more abundance and choice for consumers, who in turn exercised their power of selection. This drove competitors to further elevate their offerings and change their business models in each wave. The evolution of retail also paralleled what many economists cite as one of the most important economic shifts in history: a century-long power shift from producers to consumers—from those who make and sell to those who buy. Indeed, consumers are now the most powerful players in commerce.

Wave I, lasting roughly from 1850 to 1950, is known as the era of "producer power," when demand was greater than supply and distribution was limited. Thus, consumers had to accept what was available, affording producers pricing power. As the old saying goes, "You can have whatever color Model T Ford you like as long as it is black." Every consumer sector was predominantly governed by this model—production-driven demand.

Wave II, lasting from 1950 and peaking with its impact on retailing between 1980 and 2000, was the post–World War II era of tremendous economic growth, with massive product, retail and brand expansion, facilitated by the equally rapid expansion of distribution. This growth afforded an abundant selection of goods and services for consumers, which required businesses, for the first time, to *create* demand for their offerings. Thus was born the era depicted by the television show *Mad Men*—the halcyon days of mass marketing and the golden age of advertising, with creative "geniuses" compelling consumers to desire their clients' cool brands. Wave II is defined as a marketing- and distribution-driven economy.

From a retail perspective, it was also defined by the launch of every major retail format that exists today: the big-box category killers; specialty chains; discounters; a greatly expanded department-store sector; TV retailing (i.e., HSN and QVC); and, later, e-commerce. About 70 percent of the nation's economy would become consumption driven late in "Wave II."

And now, in 2010, we are in the throes of Wave III, which we believe will prove to be retail's greatest transformation yet. As companies battle for market share, consumers have grown accustomed to an instantaneous and unlimited selection of virtually anything they might dream of. This dynamic has led to their demand for experiences over "stuff," customized products and services over mass-market or "mega" brands, real value over ostentatious "bling," constant novelty, immediate availability and, finally, product providers whose community interests and involvement trump their self-interest.

These long-gestating dynamics have now come to full fruition. The already over-used and little-understood phrases "consumer-centric," "consumer power" and "consumer century" now mean something real. The tipping point has arrived. All value-chain participants in consumer product or service industries, especially wholesalers and retailers themselves, must identify and understand these forces, and then transform their value chains accordingly.

Even at this early stage, we can identify retailers and wholesalers that are transforming their value chains for maximum control. Conversely, we can also see who has failed. (We will discuss both in the chapters to come.) Happily, the key strategic and structural characteristics of the new models required for sustainable competitive advantage become apparent when we examine the winners.

And finally, we raise and analyze the major issues and implications that this great transformation will have for all consumer-facing industries.

The Consumer Force

Our thesis starts with consumers. Now with instantaneous access to hundreds of equally compelling products and services, they have both consciously and subconsciously elevated their expectations beyond any precedent. Therefore, the traditional business strategies employed in the past are today simply the price of entry for reaching competitive parity. Adding to the competitive congestion are new distribution platforms, including the Internet, mobile electronic devices, kiosks, in-home selling events and others, all of which are accelerated by technology and globalization. These dynamics—the convergence of a new consumer paradigm and an overcrowded marketplace—have finally brought the industry to the brink of fundamental change. Those retail and consumer-facing businesses that understand these dynamics and proactively change their business models will win. Those that do not will fail.

The consumer value shifts ultimately driving the transformation did not happen overnight. Furthermore, consumers did not sit down and write a wish list of new desires. The new dynamics evolved slowly. Value creators (retailers, brands and services) identified and anticipated what innovative new value would win consumers and beat competitors. And, as consumers embraced these new offerings, they raised the value bar. This process continues today.

While this interplay might appear simple, we believe there are some profound strategic and structural shifts occurring among winning retailers, brands and services that are conspicuously absent among the losers.

We further believe that there is a commonality in these shifts, not yet articulated, that will lead to a cohesive picture of a new and winning business model.

In Search of the Thread

We identified a mix of retailers, brands and services from different industries serving various consumer segments. Then, through research, conversations with consumers and with top executives, we explored the major strategic and structural changes the companies were implementing to satisfy shifting consumer desires.

Following is a partial list of retailers and brands that we evaluated: Costco, Wal-Mart, Kohl's, Zappos, Starbucks, Home Shopping Network, VF Corporation (The North Face, Vans, Reef, Wrangler and other brands), Ralph Lauren, J. Crew, lululemon, Macy's, Sears, JCPenney, Apple, P&G, Pepsi-Cola, Best Buy, Circuit City, Linens 'N Things, Cabella's, Abercrombie & Fitch, RadioShack, The Gap, Whole Foods, Trader Joe's, Target and Zara.

In every single case, the "obvious" was obvious, and not at all profound. Every one of them, including the failing ones, insisted that, at its core, it was "consumer-centric." Well, naturally! Each articulated that it knew its target demographic, had conducted segmentation (in many cases on a psychographic basis [attitudes, etc.]), had conducted frequent focus groups and was relentlessly responding to its consumers' needs.

And a snapshot of key brand promises relative to their core consumer expectations would confirm that they *do* understand and *have* been meeting expectations: Costco, the "discovery" of something new every day; Wal-Mart, "save more, live better"; Kohl's, convenience; Zappos, service; Starbucks, the "third place"; HSN, "where you are"; The North Face, "never stop exploring"; Ralph Lauren, be "Gatsby"; J. Crew, "cool"; lululemon, "creating components for people to live a longer, healthier, more fun life"; Macy's, "magic of"; JCPenney, "every day matters."

This understanding of their core consumers was certainly a common strategic thread. And, accordingly, all these companies declared their intention of continually elevating the shopping experience and innovating, whether in-store or online. Speaking of which, another common thread related to the first was that they also put the use of being online at the top of their strategic priority list.

In fact, each company (again, in varying degrees), including Circuit City and Linens 'N Things, could articulate how well positioned and dominant its brands were, at least in their own minds. They could all expand on their clear value propositions, and explain why they were cost competitive, efficiently productive, superior supply chain managers and marketers, etc.

These rather redundant observations simply confirmed what we believed to be a truism: namely, that all businesses must excel in operations on all these fronts in the consumer-driven Wave III or they would soon be dead.

It did not take us long to realize that these commonalities among winners and losers could be found in any textbook or the thousands of available business books. And indeed, had we not been able to discover a more profound thread, then this book would likely not have been published. The world doesn't need another business book espousing the obvious.

The obvious is not to be dismissed lightly, however. At the very least, successful businesses must excel in executing all these strategic imperatives, so by definition they are important. What we are saying is that all these strategic operating principles are simply the "price of entry" to achieve competitive parity. They may get the business to the playoffs, but there must be something more strategically powerful to win the championship.

Furthermore, the fact that Circuit City and Linens 'N Things believed they were operating on all those strategic principles right up to their slide into bankruptcy—and they certainly weren't the only ones in that situation—supported our hunch that there was a more profound thread connecting the winners.

So we dug deeper.

Reaching for the Revelation

As we read between the lines in both written materials and conversations, we discovered two subtle yet important differences among the winners: first, a greater intensity to continually probe their consumers' behavior and desires in order to achieve a deeper, more emotional connection with them; and second, a strong focus on distribution—an understanding that in the overcompeted world of consumer products, services and retailing, they had to figure out how to get to their consumers ahead of, and more often than, their competitors.

The fact that the winners were executing better on both counts differentiated them from their lesser competitors. However, while we felt we were close to the fundamentally new thread, we weren't quite there yet. So we stepped back and tried to take a fifty-thousand-foot view of their operating models. Was there a tiered variation among the winners, the emerging winners and those in decline? We began to ask questions about some of the major strategies the winners were employing to arrive at our answer.

In our interviews with industry leaders, some themes started to emerge. One theme concerned the issue of control. Eric Wiseman, CEO of the VF Corporation, one of the world's largest apparel makers with over fifty-five brands (The North Face, Wrangler and Lee Jeans, Vans, Reef and Jansport among them), said in 2006, "[retail] will grow much more dramatically than our overall growth rate. In lifestyle brands like Vans, The North Face, and Nautica, we want to continue to present the brand in ways we can control."[1]

Ralph Lauren spoke many times over the years about controlling his own destiny, while accelerating expansion of his retail business and buying back most of his outstanding licenses, echoing the same point. His quote from his company's annual meeting in 2003—"The reason I'm excited about retailing today is that it is in our hands. We are in control of our destiny"—appeared in a year when close to 50 percent of revenues were generated by his retail business.[2] And, in those select department stores that sell his brands, why does he demand a dedicated location, largely determine line mix, size, frequency and presentation and even insert his employees to service the customers?

And there has been no one more vocal about controlling distribution over the years than J. Crew CEO Mickey Drexler. In a September 14, 2010, Goldman Sachs retail conference, he provided an exclamation point to how serious he is about such control, stating, "I don't ever want to be in a business where I don't control my distribution, period, end of sentence."

The race for private and/or exclusive brands among all traditional retailers was another clear theme that we saw, and it seemed motivated by more than just a desire for differentiation or pricing flexibility. Over 50 percent of JCPenney's apparel brands are their own. Of their eight so-called power brands—Ambrielle; a.n.a; Arizona; Cooks; Chris Madden; St. John's Bay; Stafford; and Worthington—five of them have over $1 billion each in sales. Macy's, Kohl's, Target and Wal-Mart are all accelerating their private/exclusive programs. At Safeway, Walgreens and Whole Foods, the same trend is visible. Macy's private and exclusive branding strategy has been further developed and enhanced with the "My Macy's" concept of localizing its product offerings according to local consumer preferences.

And the theme reemerged in the electronics sector when Best Buy CEO Brian Dunn commented, "We believe that when an experience touches a customer, you must own it."[3]

There were other intriguing perspectives, however. Wal-Mart's vice chairman, Eduardo Castro-Wright, said of its global and e-commerce expansions, "Customers will be able to experience the brand wherever and whenever they want."[4] Other than their obvious aggressive growth plans, was there something more strategically fundamental to be found in that statement? At HSN, Mindy Grossman said, "The days of trying to get a consumer to come to you are over. You really have to be in the consumer's world, wherever, whenever and however."[5]

Why are Pepsi and Coca-Cola acquiring the independent bottling firms that distribute their products? And, since this move centrally coordinates their many brands for marketing purposes, why do they define it as "the power of one"? Why is P&G testing its own retail stores? Why is Apple expanding its retail business, with Microsoft soon to follow?

Our answer emerged, and in our view, it has revolutionary potential.

On the Edge of the Revolution

We found that every single one of those questions could be answered by the fact that companies' success was fundamentally being driven by the degree of predominant *control* they had over their entire value chains, from creation all the way through to consumption. Some had total control, and all others were pursuing it. It didn't need to be defined by actual ownership, but control was a crucial element.

At first we said, "So what?"

Upon further investigation, we realized that higher levels of success were being realized by those who had greater control over the parts of their value chains that touch the consumer: co-creation of value (consumer input through research, tracking, etc); continuous innovation and re-creation of the consumer's desire; and distribution and final presentation to the consumer.

Again, we thought, "So what?" And then the dots connected.

Experiential Superiority

The first dot was that the most successful companies were those creating superior experiences, and constantly striving for better. And it was not confined solely to a superior product, brand or service, or just the shopping experience. We realized, for example, that when consumers simply *hear* the names of companies such as Trader Joe's, Whole Foods, Disney, Apple, Abercrombie & Fitch and others, they get excited in anticipation of both the shopping and consumption experience. In fact, we probed deeper and studied some of the new work in neurology depicting the biochemical effects in the human brain that can affect behavior, particularly consumption. We found that brands like those listed above actually trigger a chemical high in the brain. So when consumers hear the brand name, they're likely to scoot to the store or brand ahead of all competitors.

For instance, Abercrombie & Fitch and Starbucks each create a neurological experience, indelibly connecting with all five senses and the most important "sixth" sense: the mind, and the emotions it triggers. As proof of the Starbucks connection, one need only observe the long waiting line at a Starbucks in an airport right next to a Mc-Donald's (or any other coffee vendor), with no line at all. Simply providing a great product with a deep understanding of the target consumer is merely the price of entry today. The superior competitors will be providing what we are calling *neurological connectivity.*

Distributional Superiority

The second dot concerned those who had superior distribution—namely, getting their value to consumers when, where, how and how often they wanted it. These companies tended to be the most successful as well. H&M, Best Buy, Ralph Lauren and brands of the VF Corporation such as Wrangler represent such excellence in distribution.

As we explored this consumer "touch point" (point-of-sale), more deeply, we also found and defined a superior distribution concept. As we've mentioned, because of an overcrowded marketplace consumers have total access, which is accelerated by the Internet and numerous other distribution platforms. Therefore, the new level of excellence is *preemptive distribution,* or getting to the consumers ahead of the competition with precisely what they desire and where, when and how often they want to receive it.

Superior Value-Chain Control

Finally, we realized that neither neurological connectivity nor pre-emptive distribution would be possible to implement without total control of the value chain, from creation to consumption. The ability to build into the operating process a series of subtle elements that drive the neurological connectivity, capture key interactions with the consumer and feed that information back into the overall design of the product and experience is granted by control of the value chain. Similarly, the ability to rapidly evolve a multidistribution model or incorporate new technologies requires this control. Again, it's important to note that some people may misunderstand "control" to mean ownership of the entire value chain. It does not. When we analyzed the winners, we found that most had value chains that were highly collaborative between suppliers and producers. However, the value creator is in constant pursuit, either proactively or reactively, of controlling its final creation, distribution and presentation to the consumer—thus controlling the value chain. Ralph Lauren's relentless quest to manage and control his brand's entire line mix, size, frequency, presentation, sales and service into and through his department store customer's space (e.g., Bloomingdale's) is a perfect example.

Our Operating Principles

In our view, these three integrated strategic operating principles are imperative for success in Wave III. Indeed, they are revolutionary in the powerful synergy they can create not only to sustain competitive advantage, but also to achieve outsize growth.

And it is critical to understand that not one, or even two, of these principles can alone drive such success. All three must be employed, with total value-chain control being the lynchpin that makes the other two possible:

- **Neurological Connectivity:** as consumers expect total access, the retailer or brand must far exceed consumers' expectations. They must align with one, or a number of the five consumer value shifts (which we will discuss later) and co-create (with the consumer) an "experience" that indelibly connects with all five human senses and the all-powerful sixth sense: the mind. This neurological connection becomes a holistic experience, consisting of pre-shopping anticipation, shopping ecstasy and consumption satisfaction. It is not a static experience, however, and requires constant reinforcing, often with subtle and frequent changes. This connection also preempts competitors, as its creator becomes the product, brand or service of choice.

- **Preemptive Distribution:** the necessity to gain access to consumers ahead of the multiplicity of equally compelling products or services, and precisely where, when and how the consumer wants it. Preemptive distribution requires speed and the ability to reinforce the neurological connection (or brand promise). By definition, this requires an integrated and possibly rapidly changing matrix of all possible distribution mediums, including distribution into faster-growing international markets.

- **Value-Chain Control:** No consumer-facing business can achieve the highest levels of a neurological connection and preemptive distribution without complete control of its entire value chain, from creation all the way to consumption. This defines a vertically integrated (not necessarily owned), controlled business model.

These three strategic operating principles are imperative to most efficiently and effectively satisfy the relentlessly increasing demands of consumers, and thus to win share in a hypercompetitive marketplace.

Key Insights and Future Predictions

While the revolutionary transformation is just beginning, the implications of our thesis will reverberate across all consumer-facing industries tomorrow, the next day and well into the future.

Following are a few major predictions:

- 50 percent of retailers and brands will disappear.

For all the reasons encompassed by our thesis, we believe it's reasonable to conclude that there will be an enormous number of retailers and brands that will simply not be able to change their business model, and therefore will not survive into Wave III. Overall, in our estimation, 50 percent of consumer businesses will disappear.

- The ultimate collapse of the traditional retail/wholesale business model is now clearly visible.

Why is Trader Joe's winning with all its own brands? Why are Macy's and other major department stores accelerating their pursuit of private and exclusive brands, as well as "localizing" their offerings? Why are wholesale brands like Ralph Lauren, Jones NY and VF Corporation's various brands increasing their direct-to-consumer retail distribution? Why is Proctor & Gamble testing two Tide Dry Cleaner stores? Why is Microsoft now following Apple with its own retail strategy?

For the past quarter-century, the classic model of retail has increasingly become ineffective and inefficient, particularly in the department-store sector (less so in the commodity-value channels, although their similar transformation will be addressed later). Therefore, with the combination of the two major new enablers— technology and globalization—to better integrate the creation and distribution of goods and services, along with relentlessly increasing consumer demands, the more enlightened retailers and wholesalers understand they must own and/or control the creation, distribution and presentation of their value directly to the consumer.

We predict that one day as much as 80–90 percent of traditional department stores' revenues will be generated by their own private and/or exclusive brands. Conversely, we also believe that the same percentage of revenues will one day come from the retail stores of designer and strong global "power" brands.

As we predict the collapse of the traditional model, we believe the visionary retailers and wholesale brands that understand this conundrum will manage its collapse together, and convert the old model into a new. Those that do not will disappear.

- Major department, discount and big-box stores will accelerate the roll out of their smaller, free-standing, "localized" neighborhood stores.

The ongoing need for growth will favor the use of preemptive distribution, which provides greater access *to* consumers and quicker and easier access *for* consumers. Kohl's was a first mover (building its whole model around "neighborhood" convenience for the time-starved working mom), and now Best Buy, JCPenney, Bloomingdale's and even Wal-Mart are expanding their small neighborhood formats. Furthermore, most are localizing their product mix and service according to consumer preferences. We believe the other major players across all of retailing will be pursuing this strategy.

- Many department stores' private brands will be expanded through a specialty chain format, branded as "neighborhood boutiques."

Further pushing the envelope of preemptive distribution will bring this opportunity to department stores that have strong private brands. Why wouldn't JCPenney open a specialty chain of Arizona stores (and others) in neighborhood locations, particularly since their database tells it where its consumers live and what they want? Why not a chain of INC or Alfani stores from Macy's, or any one of the many designer brands owned by Target?

- Amazon will open brick-and-mortar retail "showrooms."

As headlined on the front page of *Women's Wear Daily* in 2009, a Wal-Mart executive responded to a seminar question by saying that his company's greatest fear was of Amazon's opening stores.[6] Why not? With its enormous consumer database, it could localize a showroom. For example, it could present products like apparel and beauty, since the "touchy-feely and fit" desires required in those categories cannot be satisfied online. With showroom-like stores it could showcase only the local desires as mined from its data, and create a neurological experience by using new technology that allows consumers to customize outfits that can then be ordered online or in the store and delivered to their homes. Furthermore, following in the footsteps of its traditional department-store brethren, Amazon, we believe, will also pursue a private branding strategy.

- Retail stores will become hybrid enclosed "mini-malls" for increased traffic and higher productivity.

Does Peet's Coffee & Tea shop within Raley's grocery stores create a synergy? Of course it does. How about Mango, Sephora and JCPenney or Sunglass Hut, LVMH and Macy's? What's the synergy? Both the host and joined brands are go-to brands for their core consumers, thus compelling new traffic for each. The joined brand also gains preemptive distribution to new customers geographically for a low capital investment. Why not Victoria's Secret and Soma or

Cacique (the intimate-apparel specialty retailers) and others, matching up with any one of the traditional department stores whose market share, in this category, has been declining for years?

•   "Pop-up" stores and other preemptive distribution opportunities will become proactive strategies as opposed to marketing opportunities.

Target stores initiated the concept in the 1990s, locating short-term leasable space, timed around holiday or seasonal themes, primarily for marketing and publicity purposes initially. Summer in the tony Hamptons became a three-month beach and luxury showcase for Target, which also made a lot of money. Now pop-ups are used by many brands and retailers.

How about in-home marketing events, more door-to-door and cell-phone-to-cell-phone retailing, kiosks, vending machines and retailing on wheels (an Abercrombie & Fitch truck rolling across campus)?

•   As a vital link in the value chain, communications, advertising and media industries are also driven to transform their business models.

As technological advances create an infinite number of distribution platforms for communications, products and services, including many that can literally "follow" and access individual consumers 24/7, these same innovations will allow the consumer not only to block what they do not want, but to invite or grant permission to precisely what they would welcome.

This capability is already driving a fundamental transformation of the media and advertising industries toward finitely targeting both content and distribution, and carefully measuring quality and cost of contact. All consumer-facing industries are therefore looking to a future of connecting individually with consumers. Essentially, as the former CEO of VF Corporation Mackey McDonald described it in a conversation, VF envisions defining and measuring their millions of consumers as "universes of one."

- Small, rapidly cycled niche brands will trump mega-brands.

The combination of countless brands, instantaneously available in countless distribution outlets, allows consumers to select ostensibly exclusive or customized brands. This is a major shift from the Wave II market of fewer mega-brands distributed through fewer outlets; then, consumers were more conformist in their behavior, and were actually proud to be wearing or consuming the brands shared by their friends and peer groups.

- U.S. brands, wholesalers and retailers will be acquired by Chinese manufacturers and other emerging low-cost producers of consumer products.

As people in low-cost manufacturing-based countries, particularly China, seek higher standards of living and consumption, higher wages are necessary to fuel these pursuits. This runs counter to the continuing pressures from the developed countries to drive costs even lower. Therefore, to satisfy both consumers' appetite for a better life (which increases costs) while at the same time maintaining their global competitive position as low-cost producers, management must seek ways to expand top and bottom line growth as opposed to simply driving costs (wages) lower.

This conundrum is already being addressed by the larger and more visionary producers in China. They quickly assessed that the greatest value, and thus profit, was generated at the opposite end of the value chain, the end that connected with consumption: the marketplace. And they understand that the quickest way to operate in the marketplace, and to gain those fatter margins, is to buy it. Yes, to acquire marketplace brands, retailers and services.

It's already happening. Li & Fung, the world's largest apparel-sourcing agent at $15 billion, has sixteen U.S. brands under its belt and is aggressively looking for more.

Digital World as the Unstoppable Catalyst

The revolutionary shifts we believe are coming will not only accelerate, they will be unstoppable because they are embedded in (the extendable version of) Moore's Law, which predicted that the number of components in an integrated circuit would double every year until at least 2015. Put another way, the ability of the consumer to have unlimited power in the marketplace is in large part driven by the technology advancements that we see around us. The web, social networking sites such as Twitter and Facebook and mobile phones with pricing applications are just the beginning of the new wave of technology breakthroughs that will facilitate the changes that we expound in our thesis.

Because of these advancements the value chain will be redefined and compressed. New distribution platforms will emerge. Brand messages will be controlled by the consumer. For example, P&G recently launched eStore to sell directly to its consumers. The Facebook page of Pantene is using eStore to sell special promotions to its fans. Is this the beginning of a new retail/wholesale relationship with P&G and its traditional retail customers? We believe it may very well be.

Another industry-changing breakthrough was the Kindle, which along with the Internet is driving fundamental shifts in how books, newspapers, magazines and music are published and distributed. Looking further out, for those shoppers who find searching for the right size and fit in apparel a painful task, there will be technology available online to laser-size their bodies, designed and custom-made to fit and delivered to their front door in a matter of days.

Our thesis does not attempt to predict which technologies will win or lose, but it does suggest that there is a business model and a set of organizational principles that will govern the ability of every consumer business to effectively exploit these technology trends.

Final Thoughts

We believe this book offers fresh insights, and the clear understanding and guidance all businesses need to transform and control their value chains. We hope our thinking helps you determine whether this applies (or should apply) to your company and your investments, or just provides insights into your shopping habits. We acknowledge that the thinking here is just the starting point. We do not seek certainty in our argument, for certainty is rooted in inertia, inflexibility and dogma. We seek debate and dialogue, and to explore the uncertainty of the future. For in that uncertainty we see new opportunities and endless potential.

PART 1

DEFINING THE THREE WAVES OF RETAILING

CHAPTER 1

WAVE I

UNDERSTANDING PRODUCER POWER

Wave I (1850–1950)

In the late 1800s, the population of the United States was about 60 million, spread out across 38 states, with 65 percent living on farms or in small towns. There were only a dozen or so cities that had 200,000 or more residents, and yearly national income was about $10 billion. The Wild West was still wild, even as rail was being laid to follow the migrating population.

Despite suffering from the "Long Depression"—not as deep as the Great Depression, but longer, stretching from 1873 to 1897—the country nevertheless generated enough capital to spawn the so-called Gilded Age (1865–1900), with its infamous tycoons, or robber barons, who built our railroads, drilled and distributed our oil, made our steel, launched our banking system and built the foundations of our manufacturing infrastructure. America was just beginning to understand how to harness the use of electricity and new industrial processes to accelerate production in order to provide the growing population with the products and services they really needed.

The phonograph, typewriter, telephone and electric light were invented, and after Karl Benz's invention of the first combustion engine automobile in Germany in 1886, Henry Ford created the Model T Ford, ultimately replacing horse-drawn carriages. In 1913, Ford developed the concept of the assembly line, for which he was labeled the father of mass production. By the Roaring Twenties, Ford was selling hundreds of thousands of Model Ts, and he still couldn't keep up with demand.

Compare that to today, when every household has two or three cars in the driveway, yet the Big Three—General Motors, Ford and Chrysler—are not only cutting capacity but facing potential bankruptcy.

Ford's inability to keep up with demand occurred for several reasons. During the early years of Wave I and well past the turn of the century, the period of vast industrialization, transportation and communications infrastructure building was still in its infancy. There was limited access to goods and services because supply-side growth could not keep up with growing consumer demand, exacerbated by an embryonic and fragmented distribution structure and a continuously migrating population, both east to west and rural to urban. Moreover, even when there was sufficient supply, its distribution was at best uneven and inefficient, and at worst nonexistent.

It was also during this time—which is considered, not coincidentally, the beginning of America's rise to global economic dominance—that two dominant retail distribution models were conceived: the mail-order catalog and the department store.

Sears and Montgomery Ward in Wave I

Following a brief stint in the watch business, Richard Sears partnered with Alvah Roebuck in 1886 to form the classic American retailer Sears, Roebuck and Co. By 1895 they were heavily into the mail-order business, primarily targeting farmers and small-town residents, who made up the majority of the population during that period, and had limited access to stores. And while Sears was actually formed later than the first such catalog, Montgomery Ward, founded by Aaron Ward in 1872, the Sears catalog would grow bigger and also succeed longer. Monkey Wards, as its competitor was affectionately called, succumbed to the marketplace challenges of Wave II, which we will discuss later.

These catalogs demonstrated a brilliant distribution strategy: placing their "store" and all their products directly in the living rooms of all those farmers and people scattered across the country in small towns. These were people who needed things and had no other place to get them. In the truest sense of the old adage "Location, location, location," these catalogs were in the consumer's face, in his living room, faster and more frequently than their monthly treks from the farm to the general store in a town many miles away. Indeed, these companies' vision of bringing their value to the consumer was one of retailing's early and competitively innovative distribution strategies.

The Sears catalog would eventually grow to over five hundred pages, offering everything from the cradle you rocked your babies in to the coffin you were buried in. You could even buy a ready-made home with everything in it.

Today, of course, the Internet is the new catalog; however, it is not a replacement for the "old," but one of many additional distribution platforms: mobile electronic devices, kiosks, vending machines, airport stores, door-to-door selling, in-home selling events and ubiquitous stores on virtually every corner, to name a few. We live in an age of consumers having total accessibility. Therefore retail success can no longer be just about "location, location, location."

In the early 1920s, as the population began migrating from farms to small towns, Sears and Montgomery Ward, continuing their distribution strategy of following the consumer, began open-ing stores in those towns. Now they had a multichannel distribu-tion strategy, with both catalog and stores, and also a unique competitive advantage of offering high-quality essentials for fair and credible prices. They thus positioned themselves as the go-to stores for the growing middle class, a niche not competed for by the big-city department stores.

The Department Stores: "Build It and They Will Come"

In 1846, an Irish-American entrepreneur named Alexander Turney Stewart founded a soft goods store called the Marble Palace, which sold European goods. Later, it would evolve into Stewarts depart-ment store, selling apparel, accessories, carpets, glass and china, toys and sports equipment.

In 1856, Marshall Field & Company was launched in Chicago. In 1858, Macy's was founded in New York City, followed by B. Alt-man, Lord & Taylor, McCreary's and Abraham & Straus. John Wanamaker founded Wanamaker's in Philadelphia in 1877. Zion's Cooperative Mercantile Institution (ZCMI) was opened in Salt Lake City in 1869, and became the first incorporated department store in 1870. Hudson's opened in Detroit in 1881, and Dayton's in 1902 in Minneapolis.

These and many others, which grew out of small general stores at the same time that their small towns became cities, would be-come the most dominant retail segment until well into Wave II (generally defined as 1950–2000).

These Wave I department stores were called "cathedrals" and "palaces of consumption" at the time. They became daylong outing destinations for families, at first because of their breadth of offer-ings, and later because of the additional sponsored entertainment, kids' events, fashion shows, restaurants and more. Many of these palaces were also architecturally beautiful, using new building materials, glass technology and new heating, among other innovations.

Indeed, the often-misquoted line from the movie *Field of Dreams,* "If you build it, they will come," perfectly describes the juxtaposition between the department-store distribution strategy and Sears' and Ward's original distribution model of following, and bringing their value *to,* the consumer.

We need look no further than the current overstored, overstuffed retail landscape to see how these original department stores have evolved into what might more accurately be called big stores loaded with so much stuff that it's a daunting challenge for consumers. The contrast illuminates how the scarcity of competition and growing demand in Wave I provided these stores with enough pricing power, and therefore profit margins, to be able to afford all the compelling amenities that made them not just stores, but entertainment destinations.

The shifting balance between supply and demand, and how it drives changes in retail distribution models, is fundamental to our thesis, as we follow retail's evolution through Waves II and III. Just as the Sears and Montgomery Ward catalogs and early department stores were innovative new distribution models responding to the supply-and-demand equation of the time and real consumer needs, so too were their successors.

Ramping Up to Wave II

Despite the Great Depression, the overall period during Wave I, from the early 1900s through World War II, was one of positive economic growth, particularly because of industrialization. The huge expansion of highways and railroads—indeed, of all transportation and communications—marked the birth of a modern distribution infrastructure, all centered on the growing population and its migration to the cities and suburbs.

Fueled by the growing use of innovative processes, assembly-line manufacturing and electricity, the supply side of the economy (products and services) could finally try to catch up with consumer demand. There was tremendous growth in housing, new household appliances and, of course, automobiles. All this growth would survive the severe downturn of the Great Depression, and would presage the truly explosive growth after World War II and during Wave II.

Meanwhile, the retail industry continued its inexorable march in its ramp up to Wave II. In 1902, James Cash Penney launched JCPenney, which would be incorporated in 1913. While initially offering only soft goods, and without catalog distribution, JCPenney quickly became a fierce competitor of both Sears and Montgomery Ward, with all three rapidly opening stores in small towns and suburbs, chasing after the growing American middle class. JCPenney, like its predecessors, offered high-quality basic products for a good value. This value model was exactly what enabled all three competitors to continue growing even through the Depression.

Following World War II and the subsequent explosive economic growth, Sears expanded upon its distribution strategy, following the migration of consumers to the suburbs. Sears arguably built and anchored the first regional malls, leading the way for rivals like JCPenney, Macy's, McRae's and Dillard's, all of which would eventually anchor the rapidly expanding number of suburban shopping malls. And, to further solidify its domination of the niche, Sears vertically integrated and began to develop its own private brands (such as DieHard batteries, Kenmore appliances and Craftsmen Tools) and localized distribution, long before those concepts entered general practice.

This is the juncture, late in Wave I, when Sears began surging past its primary competitor, Montgomery Ward, which refused to enter the malls, considering it too costly. This would prove to be a fatal misstep, and the beginning of Ward's long slide downward.

So Sears' proactive response to the changing world around it allowed a long and powerful rise. By the early 1970s, it was one of the eight largest corporations, and one of the most powerful brands, in the world, with revenue higher than the next four retailers combined. Indeed, it was more dominant, and had greater momentum, than Wal-Mart does today.

The Downward Slide

But ultimately, like Montgomery Ward, Sears also failed to see, understand and respond to the changing economic, consumer and competitive environments outside its own four walls. Sears took a great risk and reinvented its business model, but it failed to strengthen it. In many ways, the decline of Sears can be traced back almost exactly to the day it moved into financial services, with then CEO Edward Telling's acquisition of brokerage house Dean Witter, and his infamous claim that consumers should purchase their "stocks and socks" under one roof. This inability to evolve their model to suit the times caused Sears to slip into decline. The historically savvy retailer lost its unique connection with its own consumers, delivering something they neither expected nor desired.

Ironically, latecomer JCPenney *did* evolve its business model, essentially adopting Sears' strategic advantages, such as private branding and distribution. And unlike its onetime nemesis, it has strengthened and adjusted its model to respond to the changing economic and consumer driving forces. As a result, JCPenney is currently thriving in Wave III.

It is tragic that Sears allowed its strategic advantages to dissipate. The same advantages that made it the biggest and best retailer are inherent in some of the winning retail specialty chains today, such as Abercrombie & Fitch or Zara. These stores vertically control their value chains from product development to manufacturing, operations, logistics, marketing, distribution, and the point-of-sale; therefore, they can develop their own brands and deliver the shopping experience the consumer expects from the brand. Such control also allows them greater access to, and therefore more effective distribution to, their consumers.

Sears and Montgomery Ward represent just two of many retailers whose business models and consumer value propositions were innovative and relevant to the consumer and economic environment at the time of their inception. They also evolved their competitive advantages, growing to occupy relatively dominant positions in the marketplace. However, they would ultimately represent the many chains that, after achieving such success, failed, for myriad reasons, to continue adjusting to the ever-changing economic and consumer conditions around them. Arguably, Sears' "stocks and socks" strategy was its attempt at changing its business model to adapt to the times. What it viewed as a strategy, however, turned out to be a poorly executed tactic.

Therefore, many of these historically iconic retailers simply vanished overnight, and others, such as Sears, slipped into a lengthy decline.

Chapter Highlights

We have aptly framed the evolution of retailing as the "Three Waves of Retailing." Wave I spans the time period from 1850 to 1950, Wave II from 1950 to about 2000 and Wave III, the third and in our opinion final wave, covers the period from 2000 to 2010.

As we depict each wave, we will describe the economic situation during that wave, including the supply-and-demand relationship, the competitive situation, the business strategies necessary for successful response to consumer demands and the business structure or models necessary to execute the strategies.

Wave I Key Market Characteristics

- **Production/Retail Driven:** Pricing power resided with manufacturers and retailers due to a dearth of competitors, minimum and uneven level of products and services and a fragmented or nonexistent distribution infrastructure. Therefore, consumers had to accept what was available to them.

- **Production Chasing Demand:** Producers and distributors, including retailers, were all growing and expanding to chase and capture business from shifting consumer markets. With some exceptions, notably in the larger cities, supply would continue to underserve demand, primarily due to the growth of the population, including immigrants, and the migration of the citizenry from east to west and north to south, and from rural areas to small towns and cities, all challenging an embryonic, fragmented and inefficient distribution infrastructure.

- **Single Product Specific Brands vs. Cross Categories:** Lack of cohesive marketing and communications infrastructure, as well as a scarcity of producers, resulted in both a limited availability of brands and their confinement to single product categories.

- **Fragmented, Isolated Markets:** Geographically dispersed, largely rural and small-town markets, many isolated and unconnected by transportation and/or communications; therefore the distribution of goods and services, including to retailers, was at best slow, random and inefficient.

- **Fragmented Marketing:** Due to the dispersed and isolated market structure, and the lack of a national communications and media infrastructure, advertising, sales and marketing of any type was sporadic, local, infrequent and inefficient.

Dominant Retail Models

- Freestanding department stores in cities ("palaces of consumption"), expanding later in Wave I to anchor the emerging shopping malls
- Sears' and Montgomery Ward's mail-order catalogs (as responsive distribution to rural and small towns), and in the early 1920s launching stores in small towns
- Sears constructed and anchored the first malls to be followed by department stores and JCPenney (founded in 1902) as additional anchors as they all raced toward Wave II and the mid-twentieth century

CHAPTER 2

WAVE II

LEARNING ABOUT
DEMAND CREATION IN A
MARKETING-DRIVEN ECONOMY

Capitalism Unbound

"Capitalism unbound" is certainly an apt description of the economic dynamics in the United States post–World War II and through the late 1970s. There was explosive growth across all industries, encouraged by the massive building of the nation's communications, transportation, distribution and marketing infrastructures, including retailing and all other consumer-facing industries.

Arguably, the war was the final and key factor in pulling the economy out of the Great Depression, thanks to the sheer magnitude of the effort in gearing up for global battle, both in dollars and manpower. Essentially, this effort reflated the economy. By 1945, the United States represented about 45 percent of worldwide GDP, way up from its historic norm of 25–28 percent. (Sadly, of course, this was also heightened by the economic devastation of much of the rest of the world.)

More important, the accelerated industrialization required to feed the war effort led to many innovations and advancements for the postwar commercial economy, by increasing both government and private investments in research and development in conjunction with academia. Advances in nuclear energy grew out of the war's Manhattan Project. Innovations in the aerospace industry were enormous: in 1958, the first commercial jet crossed the Atlantic. Radar and FM networks were war inventions. And there were many more.

From Pent-Up Demand to "The American Dream"

Of course, all this innovation and growth could not have happened without an equally precipitous increase in demand. And it was certainly there. Coming out of the Great Depression and World War II, American consumers had an enormous, pent-up desire for a better quality of life. They aspired beyond just necessities to products, services and surroundings that would satisfy their dreams. In fact, it was during this fertile period that the phrase "the American Dream" was coined. The goal of having a family, a home, a car in every driveway, a steady job with benefits, a college education and all other things wonderful, would be realized for millions of Americans. The new suburbia and planned communities were exemplified by Levittown in New York in the 1950s, providing tenth-of-an-acre-sized slices of the American dream to homeowners.

Leave It to Beaver, Ozzie and Harriett, The Ed Sullivan Show and many other popular TV shows of the time mirrored the Rockwellian ideal of the tranquil families watching television together in their living rooms.

Yet if you looked outside those cozy living rooms into the undercurrents of American life, you could see the emergence of social, political and cultural trends that would have a major long-term impact on America as it ramped up to the twenty-first century. Second-wave feminism, the counterculture and its resonance at Woodstock and the recognition of teens as a viable and independent cultural and economic force were among the trends changing the country. The invention of birth-control pills offered a true basis for women's freedom and independence. The civil rights movement would be as big a step for mankind as was landing on the moon. The communist panic of the 1950s and the Korean War would be followed by the Vietnam war in the 1960s, and the political and social upheavals surrounding it would mark the era, as would President Nixon's resignation. This period had many significant events, including the Cold War and the near triggering of a nuclear holocaust as the United States declared a blockade of the island of Cuba, setting the stage for the first direct face-off with the nuclear-armed Soviet Union.

All these transformative events, so enormous in their impact, did not disrupt or even slow people's determination to pursue and capture at least a slice of the American Dream.

Wave II in the United States brought not only unprecedented economic growth, but also a huge jump in Americans' standard of living. It was a virtuous cycle of plentiful jobs providing discretionary income, driving the need for more production, driving the need for more jobs, driving more demand and more spending and so forth. Life was good. Life was simple. The message to the American people was clear: Work hard, be good and the dream will come true.

The Dream Begets Mass Markets, Mass Marketing and a Massive New Distribution Infrastructure

Another key factor that made the dream possible was massive marketing and distribution systems. As more and more consumers chased the dream, they were forming enormous new markets. Conversely, equally large product and service marketers were developing new and innovative ways to market and distribute to these consumers. Two phrases were coined to accurately describe the new market dynamics in this booming economic period: "mass markets" and "mass marketing." After all, if living the good life was the American consumer's dream, mass markets, and their infinite potential for sales and profits, were the capitalist's dream.

In order to serve the enormous and growing marketplace, businesses needed a vast national distribution infrastructure. This infrastructure had to be both physical, for the distribution of products and services, and strategic, for the distribution of communications, marketing and advertising. Wave II witnessed explosive growth in highway, air, rail and sea transportation, as well as the creation of multiple channels of retail distribution. And, for mass marketers, this was the golden age of advertising and national brand creation, facilitated by the emergence of "big media": nationwide access to television and the formation of the national broadcasting channels; the national consumer print media, including specialty niche magazines; catalogs; and billboards and direct-marketing mediums.

From a retail perspective, the Federal-Aid Highway Act of 1956 was a huge catalyst for all that followed. It played a key role in population migration (from rural to urban and suburban), increased mobility and helped to establish our dominant automotive industry, new retail models and the physical distribution of goods. The irony was that the original intent behind the construction of the massive U.S. interstate highway system, a huge matrix of 45,572 miles of road, was national security. Fortunately, as it turned out, the United States never had to use it for evacuations or to mobilize troops to defend its borders against attack. However, its timing was perfect to pave the way for the explosive growth of suburbia, quickly followed by an accelerated expansion of shopping centers and large regional malls. Before World

War II, there were about eight such centers. By 1970, there were four thousand.

This vast matrix of highways, centers and malls, combined with automobiles and cheap gas to get to them, also accelerated the growth of national and regional retail chains. Most expansive were the traditional department stores, Sears and JCPenney, which realtors incentivized with attractive lease arrangements to "anchor" the malls, as consumer-drawing traffic builders. These malls were also to become home to many of the newly minted apparel specialty chains, the innovative branded retail model launched in the 1960s, which was exemplified by such pioneers as Merry-Go-Round, Esprit and Gap.

Also during this period, Sam Walton had a vision that small-town America needed basic products of great value for low prices. Thus Wal-Mart was launched. Its small-town target was different from Kmart's positioning in suburban shopping centers. Growing out of the S.S. Kresge stores founded in 1899 and the first discounter, Kmart was launched in 1962 in suburban Detroit. Target Stores was birthed in 1962 by its parent Dayton-Hudson Department Stores. And, it was positioned as a more "upscale" discounter, carrying products and brands at a price point level just above Wal-Mart and Kmart. Later, of course, it became known as standing for "cheap chic." And in Wave II, the big-box retailers (so-called category killers) such as Toys "R" Us, Circuit City and Home Depot were born.

These value/discount Wal-Mart models and the big-box category killers were massive distribution machines. Indeed, the category killers intended to do just what their name suggests—to eliminate all competitors by carrying everything in one product category (such as toys, electronics, sporting or home goods), the full spectrum of what any consumer would ever need, for volume-driven low prices.

These category-killer models and the branded apparel specialty chains, all specializing in single-product categories, along with the new discounters delivering basic, more commoditized goods, all began to win over a large share of traditionally loyal department store customers. Their lower cost structures allowed more competitive pricing, which, combined with specialized products and services, gave these new retail models a great advantage.

So, while the department stores had the distinction of being palaces of consumption and highly enjoyable shopping experiences during Wave I, they were now facing two major strategic issues that would begin to erode their market share: one, competing on price against the lower cost structures of the new emerging competitors; and two, competing against the specialists, all of whom were taking share in their focused niches from the complex array of the department stores' offerings (ultimately they would shed entire product categories such as electronics, appliances, toys and many others). As Wave II evolved, the pressure to reduce their operating costs began forcing the department stores to cut back on amenities, service and entertainment—the very things that had made them compelling destinations in Wave I.

JCPenney, Sears and Montgomery Ward were especially challenged by the discounters and category killers because their own value propositions were also founded on offering basic products for great value. Their customers, therefore, were the easiest prey for the new models. While JCPenney, Sears and Ward's all originally targeted smaller, underserved middle-class towns and suburbs, JCPenney and Sears continued their expansion into the malls and shopping centers of Wave II, while Ward's made the strategically fatal decision not to do so. It would begin to fail in the late 1970s, and totally closed what was left of its retail and catalog operations in 2001.

Though Sears spearheaded and built many of the early centers and malls, rising to its preeminent position as the largest retailer in the world by the mid-1970s, it ignored the new competitors, discounters and specialists alike, that were chipping share away from every category of its business. It did not remain responsive to the changing consumer environment. Consequently, Sears continued to operate with a relatively high cost structure, failed to shed categories in which it had lost competitive advantage and began its descent in the early 1980s. Today it is at the edge of collapse. Whether its dire situation can be turned around has been the subject of many case studies and expert discussions throughout the industry and academia. We examine it more closely in chapter 12.

JCPenney expanded both its locations, into the centers and malls, as well as its product offerings, adding furniture, electronics and sporting goods. Essentially it converted itself into a full-service department store, albeit still serving the mid-markets. Unlike Sears, JCPenney responded to the market pressures, and later in Wave II and Wave III it shed the many categories being picked off by the killers, specialty chains and discounters.

As a result of the launching of these innovative new retail models, a growing economy, increased mobility, nationwide population shifts and massive new marketing and distribution systems, the latter part of Wave II would also mark the beginning of the department store sector's steady decline, culminating in its current low level in Wave III.

Wave II as we have defined it will likely be viewed historically as the period of "nationalization" in the United States: the interconnecting of a huge national matrix of communications, transportation, distribution and marketing, all facilitating the creation, marketing and distribution of national brands, products and services, as well as national retail chains.

The Beginning of "Competitive Congestion" (Market Saturation)

As we've seen in this chapter, the American Dream for consumers also became the American Dream for producers, suppliers, marketers and retailers—until it wasn't.

As more and more competitors emerged across all consumer-facing industries, and existing companies grew larger, markets during the early 1980s became saturated. This saturation affected everything from retail to automobiles; airlines; consumer package goods; services; travel; leisure and entertainment; virtually the entire economy. This competitive congestion began to drive disequilibrium in supply and demand and a shift in power from producers to consumers. Simply put, because of increasing supply and more efficient distribution, consumers gained greater access, and therefore improved selection. So they began forcing competitors to add more value, innovate and differentiate. The market had matured to the point that consumers needed more dream-compelling reasons to purchase one competitor's offering over another.

While in production-driven Wave I, producers couldn't make or distribute products and services fast enough to satisfy demand, they now had to figure out how to *create* demand—how to compel consumers to choose them. "If you build it, they will come" was giving way to the new consumer chorus: "Give me a compelling reason to come to your store or to buy your brand." Accordingly, power in the marketplace was shifting from the supply side to the demand side; from producers, service providers and retailers to consumers.

This major paradigm shift for all consumer-facing industries, from a production-driven economy to a marketing-driven economy, meant that marketing not only became the primary strategic driver across the entire marketplace, it also drove an enormous expansion and spawned whole new businesses in the advertising, media and communications industries.

Known as the golden age of advertising, Wave II was arguably the most commercially creative era in American history. If consumers demanded compelling reasons to buy brands, they would get them in spades.

A Golden Age: The Rise of
Innovation, Branding and Advertising

The spiraling up of the American Dream was fueled by the dual forces of consumers' desire for new, more and better, and consumer-facing industries' ingenuity in creating new, more and better products and services.

However, the real engine driving this growth, and the engine necessary to create demand for one's product or service, was marketing—more specifically, branding and advertising.

You could see product promotion on ABC, NBC and CBS, and in *Time, Sports Illustrated, Life, Look, Colliers,* the *Saturday Evening Post, Glamour, Cosmopolitan,* and so on. Deeper into Wave II (during the 1970s and '80s), segmented marketing was born, supported by special-interest magazines like *Ebony, Rolling Stone, Mad, Jet, National Lampoon* and others.

Big brands were expanding nationwide, and new brands were sprouting almost daily: P&G, RJ Reynolds, Coca-Cola, Levi's, Oldsmobile, Ford, Timex, Playtex, Pabst Blue Ribbon, Cheerios, Esprit, Gap and hundreds more.

Finally, this era marked the emergence of the biggest engines of all: the now-iconic advertising agencies, big and small, that arguably created the cleverest, funniest, sincerest and most compelling messages to consumers in America's history.

DDB, BBD&O, Ogilvy & Mather, J. Walter Thompson, Leo Burnett, Grey Advertising, McCann Erickson, Ted Bates & Co., Wells Rich Greene and Kenyon & Eckhardt were but a few of the giants of that era. Together they turned out such legendary ads and slogans as the Marlboro Man, VW's Beetle, "Nothing gets between me and my Calvins," "I'd walk a mile for a Camel," "Winston tastes good like a cigarette should," "Hey Mabel, Black Label," "Fall into the Gap," "It's the real thing," and "Flick my Bic," among others.

In retailing, the Gap began its meteoric rise from a little shop in San Francisco selling Levi's Jeans to the largest branded apparel retailer in the world. Others, such as Esprit, have diminished in their American presence, but remain strong international brands. A third group, including Merry-Go-Round (one of the first specialists), is no longer in business at all.

Interestingly, the success or failure of these early specialists was all a result of how they operationally executed our three strategic principles. At their inception, it's unlikely they would have defined their models on those principles, or they might have articulated them differently. However, with or without their understanding, the specialty business models were, and still are, the quintessential example of our thesis.

Ralph Lauren: A Wave II Visionary

Among the iconic national brands being launched almost daily, and existing brands being built to enormous scales, a true branding visionary emerged during the 1960s: Ralph Lauren. Most brands during Wave I and well into Wave II were single-product category brands, like Levi's Jeans, Tide soap, Lucky Strike cigarettes and so forth. All these great brands spent millions of dollars on marketing, advertising and publicity, pushing their single-product message about the product's actual benefits into consumers' minds.

Ralph Lauren's brand, on the other hand, did not emanate from a product. It grew out of his vision of a "Gatsby-like" world where he and his brand would play a dominant role. As seen in his advertising, and even in his headquarters on Manhattan's Madison Avenue, the entire imagery of his brand powerfully communicates that lifestyle. Lauren's brand emanated from his dream of an elegant and sophisticated world in which hundreds of elegant and sophisticated people, from men to women to children, are all using hundreds of elegant and sophisticated products, all branded Ralph Lauren. Thus, rather than slapping his name on a bunch of different products, he attached his name to a lifestyle, which represented the dream he wanted to share with his customers.

Another macroshift in Wave II, then, was the shift from single-product brands like Levi's Jeans to Ralph Lauren's enormously successful brand, which was arguably the first lifestyle apparel brand. Thus began the power of the perceived or emotional benefits that a brand could offer consumers, which would eventually supersede tangible product benefits such as fit, price, performance, etc. Put another way, Ralph Lauren was the first to use the power of dreams to create demand for a brand, compelling consumers away from the single-product-driven competition.

For example, when you hear or read the brand name Levi's, you think of blue jeans. When you hear or read the brand name Ralph Lauren or Polo, it conjures up all kinds of Gatsby-esque images in your mind, almost like a movie that you dream of being in. And since his brand's inception over fifty years ago, the pictures used in his advertising have done their job—coaxing countless consumers to enter the Ralph Lauren lifestyle and buy it all, from Polo pants to Polo paint.

Thus, in Wave II, Ralph Lauren launched a new model for branding called lifestyle brands, which were superior in two respects to single-product-category brands like Levi's Jeans: first, a lifestyle permits the brand to offer multiple products provided they fit the brand's particular lifestyle positioning (from pants to paint, yet both within the same imagery); and second, a lifestyle permits the brand to create products for all consumer segments, from men to women and children, provided they fit the brand's lifestyle depiction.

Put another way, Ralph Lauren created a picture of a Gatsby-like life into which he could insert virtually any product as long as it was suitably Gatsby-like (in his interpretation). Conversely, Levi's created blue jeans and put them into pictures (ads) that they spent millions of dollars on, for about a hundred years, indelibly burning into the minds of their consumers that the Levi's brand stands for blue jeans.

In fact, despite numerous attempts over many years of attaching its brand to sportswear, jackets and other products in an attempt to reposition the brand as a lifestyle, Levi's remains a blue jean brand, even with its chain of retail stores that sell other casual-wear items.

Marvin Traub's Blomingdale's: A Retail Game-Changer

If Ralph Lauren was a lifestyle brand visionary, Marvin Traub, the CEO of Bloomingdale's during Wave II, was his equal on the retail side. In fact, it was Marvin who gave Ralph his start by allowing the "lifestyle" presentation of Ralph's line in arguably the first shop-in-shop in the department-store industry.

Also, Bloomingdale's broke new ground in elevating the shopping experience, initiating a strategy of creating a continuous series of themed events during the 1980s, many of them based on the cultures of countries around the world. For example, a Mediterranean Odyssey was one of many such themes kicked off by black-tie parties; attended by local and national luminaries; and featuring indigenous products, fashions and artifacts from the various Mediterranean countries. Some of these promotions lasted a month or longer and turned its 59th Street store in Manhattan into kind of an experiential bazaar.

It was this kind of Marvin Traub game-changing vision that gave credence to its advertising slogan: "Bloomingdale's: Like No Other Store in the World."

The Bridge to Wave III

Another interesting take on Wave II, one that business leaders of the time would likely agree on, is that it was a time when conducting business was actually *fun*—because there was real, organic

growth. While competition was heavy, markets were not oversaturated to the extent they would be in Wave III, when the battle for
market share in a slow-to-no-growth economy would become fe-
rocious. Indeed, in Wave II, the ad guys on Madison Avenue could
enjoy a three-martini lunch with clients and still make their numbers. In Wave III, they would be lucky to squeeze in a sandwich at
their desks while working ten-hour days just to keep up with the
competition.

In closing the chapter on Wave II, we reemphasize the forces
that drove this period of enormous and unprecedented growth. It
would not have been possible without mass marketing, advertising,
communications, distribution and all that uniquely American
brand building and demand creation.

Wave II Key Market Characteristics

- **Marketing Driven:** As the overabundance of Wave II grew
  beyond the bare needs of consumers, producers and retailers were forced to create demand, to create compelling reasons for consumers to shop at their stores and/or buy their
  brands.
- **Demand Creation:** Thus the economy, including retailing,
  shifted from being production driven and chasing demand
  in Wave I to marketing driven and creating demand in
  Wave II.
- **Lifestyle Branding:** Similarly, there was explosive growth in
  brands across all industries. Such competitive congestion
  also required brands to become more compelling, to lure
  consumers away from competitors. Lifestyle brands, the
  first of which was launched by Ralph Lauren, would therefore begin to gain an advantage over the less-compelling
  single-product brands.
- **Mass Markets:** As the population migrated to the fast-growing cities and suburbs, combined with the growth of the

communications, distribution and marketing infrastructures to serve these huge markets, the term "mass markets"
was coined.

- **Mass Marketing:** Accordingly, with the launch of television
  and the national broadcast and print media, as well as similarly explosive growth in advertising and other forms of
  communications, the apt description "mass marketing" was
  attached to Wave II.

Dominant Retail Models

- Major expansion of national chains across all of retailing,
  including department stores
- Sears and JCPenney as anchors to strip and regional malls
- Launch and accelerated growth of apparel specialty retail-
  ing chains
- Launch of Kmart, Wal-Mart and Target
- Launch of big-box retailing such as Toys "R" Us, Home
  Depot and Circuit City

CHAPTER 3

WAVE III

THE FINAL SHIFT TO
TOTAL CONSUMER POWER

On The Edge of Transformation

Wave III marks the final phase of one of the most important economic shifts in history—"an enormous global power shift from producers to consumers, from those who make, to those who buy," says Professor Rosabeth Moss Kanter of the Harvard Business School.[1] The enormity of that statement points to a new consumer and marketplace paradigm. The power shift described by Kanter was driven by three fundamental elements.

More and Cheaper Access

According to the International Council of Shopping Centers (ICSC), the share of total retail space accounted for by the shopping-center industry has grown every year for the last thirty years (1980–2010), despite three previous recessions and now the Great Recession. There are 7.2 billion square feet of shopping center space in 2010, more than double the 3.3 billion in 1980. This figure has grown almost four times as fast as the average 1 percent rate of population growth during the same period. There are now over 22 feet of shopping-center space for every man, woman and child in the United States. To put that in global context, Sweden is a runner-up with 3 square feet per capita.

Note that these numbers measure only the roughly 32,000 largest shopping centers of over 50,000 square feet, or 33 percent of the total gross leasable space. If the other 67 percent of small shopping centers were taken into account, total square footage in the United States would be about 13 billion, or an incredible 42 square feet per capita.[2]

One of the factors driving much of this expansion in retail space was the emergence of the "wholesale discount clubs," which were also launched in Wave III. Home Depot, Lowe's, Barnes & Noble, Best Buy, Linens 'N Things, Blockbuster and many other new category killers were born, and there was accelerated expansion of many other categories, including fast food (Starbucks, Dunkin' Donuts and countless others).

Adding to the retail expansion during this period was a massive increase in liquidity in the financial markets, much of which was used to support marginally performing stores that would otherwise have closed. Retailers' rationale for keeping these underperforming stores open was that despite their lower profitability, they still contributed minimally, while their closure would be a net reduction to growth. Furthermore, as consumer spending continued to rise, retailers reasoned that the promise of future sales would offset the current lower returns from underperforming stores.

Along with this industry-wide use of excess liquidity to maintain poorly performing stores, in pursuit of increasing share of a slow-growing and highly competitive market, retailers also used

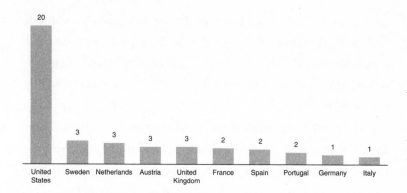

Figure 3.1: Retail saturation. The U.S. retail market is over-developed relative to other markets. *Source: Cushman & Wakefield; KSA research and analysis*

access to easy financing to open stores with lower returns on capital. In some cases—the Steve & Barry's apparel chain is the most pronounced example—entire business models were created on the basis of attractive financing arrangements that more than covered low or nonexistent operating profits.

And, of course, all these rapidly growing shopping centers and the stores within them were not empty. They were full of products and services, which also indicated that supply-side growth had outpaced demand and population growth.

Today, one need only scan through any of the major print or broadcast media, or just eyeball the seemingly infinite stream of new brands in the stores and malls, to get a sense of just how the overload of stuff has outpaced demand. A few anecdotal facts also support this imbalance. In 1980 there were about six major blue jean brands. Today, we estimate there are over eight hundred. There were about fifty major apparel brands in 1980, and our projections are that there are over four thousand today. In 1947, there were roughly twenty automobile brands in the world; today, as listed on kbb.com, (Kelley Blue Book), there are eighty five. And while worldwide production capacity for automobiles is 90 million, there is demand for only 60 million, according to the International Organization of Motor Vehicle Manufacturers. Tide soap was a mono-brand in Wave II; today, Tide.com lists thirty-nine sub-brands of Tide.

While such explosive growth in brands across all industries were obviously intended to capture a share of additional market segments, this expansion would not have been possible without globalization and the reallocation of resources worldwide, combined with new technologies and greatly increased productivity (the ability to make more for less). These dynamics facilitated the more efficient and effective distribution of the ever-increasing number of brands and services.

Quicker and Easier Access

Accelerating the growth of retail space and brands, and products and services to fill the space, was the onset of new technologies and their more sophisticated implementation, providing a multiplicity of new, more rapid and responsive distribution platforms. Internet retailing was launched (with countless sites, including the behemoth eBay) and led to the onset of mobile electronic and social network retailing. TV retailing took off, most notably with HSN and QVC. And catalogs, door-to-door sales, in-home and event marketing all continued to grow. Hundreds of new branded specialty chains were born, along with new consumer product brands and services of all types, and expansive sub-branding and licensing of brands across all consumer industries. Moreover, aided by new information technologies, consumer-facing businesses could instantaneously identify where and when demand existed as well as track sales as they happened. And the new distribution technologies enabled businesses to immediately respond and deliver to those demands. The fastest-growing retail model in Wave III was the small, independently owned "boutiques" in neighborhoods close to their consumers, according to a study conducted by the National Retail Federation (NRF). Large retailers adopted the strategy of spinning off smaller neighborhood store formats, to provide their consumers quicker and easier access.

Smarter Access

The expansion of information and communications mediums in Wave III was unprecedented, particularly the explosive growth of the Internet, which enabled consumers, with the tap of a key, to gain instant access to virtually all the information and knowledge they would ever need. There are an estimated 50 billion websites and counting. There are now hundreds of TV channels, compared to only a handful in the early years of Wave II, and myriad trade and consumer print mediums, most serving specialized niches, however arcane. Mobile electronic devices are now too numerous to count.

Consider this fact: Between 1999 and 2002, the amount of information communicated in the form of print, film, magnetic and optical storage was equivalent to 37,000 Libraries of Congress (which holds 17 million books). That amount of information is equivalent to a thirty-foot-high stack of books for each of the world's more than six billion people. Yet between 2002 and 2010, it is estimated to have grown tenfold.[3]

On a pragmatic level, shoppers can search and compare prices, quality and the performance or style of goods in a matter of minutes, which not only makes them more intelligent shoppers, but also eliminates hours of physical effort and transportation costs. While shopping in a given store, iPhones and BlackBerries enable consumers to compare the price on a product with the prices on the same product in all other stores in the area.

There is also scanning technology that scans shoppers' body dimensions for apparel, and then prints out a report advising which brands in a given mall will best fit that shopper.

Consumer Power on Steroids

Simply put, consumers now have total access to an unlimited selection of anything and everything they want. Hundreds of equally compelling retailers, products, brands or services are available at their fingertips, across the street, or delivered to their front door. And these products and services are getting newer and less expensive every day.

Because of the power of total access, consumers' behavior has changed, and they now exert total control over the marketplace. Retailers must either fulfill their deepest desires or the consumers will walk out the door to a competitor across the street, tap into another website or access any one of hundreds of equally compelling products or services. Welcome to Wave III!

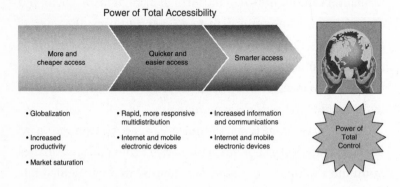

Figure 3.2: Power of total accessibility

CHAPTER 4

WAVE III

THE TRANSFORMATION

With instantaneous and unlimited access to virtually anything they might be dreaming of, consumers are capitalizing on their new-found power with full force. They are defining value for themselves differently. They are elevating their desires to the final level of "self-actualization," as defined in Abraham Maslow's "Hierarchy of Needs."[1] The theory postulated that as each level of human needs was fulfilled, we would move up to the next level. Thus, as basic physiological needs were satisfied, safety would be the next motivator, followed by social needs, esteem needs, and finally, self-actualization.

There was a marked increase in wealth during the last quarter of the twentieth century that paralleled the abundance of stuff for consumers to spend it on. The U.S. Census Bureau reported that from 1980–2010, the median U.S. household income grew from about $36,000 to close to $50,000.[2] In fact, as the United States outsourced much of its production across all industries to underdeveloped and emerging countries, many economists declared that the ceding of the U.S. production base transformed the economy from one of value creation to one of value consumption, further adding to consumer power. Consumption as a percentage of GDP (gross domestic product) rose from 62 percent during Wave II to over 70 percent in Wave III. This has caused a fundamental shift in how consumers are now seeking and defining happiness and satisfaction. Judging from numerous studies that find there is no correlation between the increase of wealth and a corresponding increase in happiness, one can conclude that consumers are sated with, and perhaps even turned off to, "stuff."

The same holds true in other developed countries. In Japan, for example, between 1958 and 1987 there was a fivefold increase in real income and no increase in average self-reported "happiness."[3] And, in the United States, according to a 2002 study by Ed Diener and Robert Biswas-Diener, *Social Indicators,* once household income reaches $50,000, happiness levels plateau, even compared to households with an income of over $90,000.[4]

Therefore, while increased wealth may lead to increased purchasing, it does not buy happiness or satisfaction. In fact, as a recent study reveals, additional material possessions rarely create any lasting joy for individuals. "Individuals adapt to material goods, and . . . material goods yield little joy for most individuals. . . . Material goods have little effect on well-being above a certain level of consumption . . . people's aspirations adapt to their possibilities and the income that people say they need to get along rises with income."[5]

As suggested, then, it is Maslow's broadly defined term "self-actualization" that now holds the key to consumers' happiness and well-being. This strongly suggests that consumers will be apt to spend more of their wealth on experiences rather than things.

Metrics in support of this major shift in consumer behavior from stuff to services (which includes experiences) and "self-actualization" can be seen on the accompanying chart.

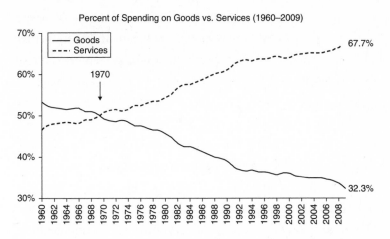

Figure 4.1: Spending on goods vs. services from 1960 to 2009. *Source: Bureau of Economic Analysis; NEA data*

As consumers seek higher states of well-being, there have been five major consumer value shifts from Wave II to Wave III:

- From needing stuff to demanding experiences (the "clubby" Abercrombie and Fitch experience trumps buying pants off of a department store shelf, and the Apple store turns computer shopping on its head)
- From conformity to customization (ubiquitous megabrands like Levi's and Gap are losing to specialized, "localized" niche brands)
- From plutocracy to democracy (accessible luxury for all: Mossimo and Rowley at Target, Vera Wang at Kohl's, Nicole Miller at JCPenney, etc.)
- From wanting new to demanding new *and* now (what's new today is cloned tomorrow, favoring "fast fashion" brands like Zara that create two new lines every week, and the convenience of Internet and neighborhood stores)

- From self to community (proliferation of social networks and community interests such as sustainability initiatives are trends, no longer simply commercial promotional gimmicks)

From Needing Stuff to Demanding Experiences

With so many closets, kitchens and garages full of stuff, the appetite to keep buying more is falling dramatically. Another study, at Cornell University, measures the comparative satisfaction of material versus experiential purchases over time, and the results are startling. The level of satisfaction drops dramatically for material purchases and increases for experiential purchases. "We found that participants were less satisfied with their material purchases (than experiences) because they were more likely to ruminate about un-chosen options, tended to maximize when selecting material goods and satisfice when selecting experiences, examine un-chosen material purchases more than un-chosen experiential purchases . . . and that relative to experiences, satisfaction with their material possessions was undermined more by comparisons to other available options. Our results suggest that experiential purchase decisions are easier to make and more conducive to well-being."[6]

These studies and many more overwhelmingly suggest that consumers in pursuit of "happiness" will be acquiring more experiences. Another reason for choosing experiences is that they are co-created by provider and consumer, making their perceived value much higher than their price. Conversely, the price of goods is most often intrinsic to their physical value. For example, Abercrombie & Fitch (A&F) provides the environment of a "cool, sexy" shopping experience, and lululemon provides yoga classes. However, the consumer, at the moment he or she is in the environment, is reacting and shaping that experience to themselves, to make it complete. And not only does the uniqueness of the co-created experience elevate its value, but it is also conceptual and temporal (a one-time happening). Conversely, every day consumers can look at their "stuff" and reflect whether the car, TV, phone, or pair of jeans was really the best purchase they could have made.

Moreover, because of the temporal and individual nature of experience, the evaluation is also fleeting. It is almost impossible to systematically evaluate and compare whether the purchase of one experience was better than other options, particularly when the experience is predominantly part of the consumer's memory. Therefore, while products can be evaluated on the basis of physical and common criteria, co-created, unique experiences cannot, making the pursuit of them more anticipatory and exciting. Finally, and more significantly, consumers will pay more for an experience than they will for stuff.

Yet another perspective on too much stuff comes from Barry Schwartz's book *The Paradox of Choice: Why More is Less.*[7] He points out that "piles of stuff" in a store, while attempting to create the positive impression that there are plenty of options, actually have the opposite effect. Rather than making consumers happier with such abundance, it frustrates and exhausts them before they even begin to shop. So not only is it an unpleasant experience, it's actually a turnoff. Well-edited retail brands, on the other hand, which know their consumers' likes and dislikes, provide an emotionally connecting experience in which less is more. A good example would be Trader Joe's, where there is a more limited selection of each category than in traditional grocery stores, yet it consistently surpasses its consumers' expectations. An often-heard remark is that "Trader Joe's knows what I want!" Another example is Lane Bryant, a sportswear specialty chain that caters to plus-size women. According to its former CEO, Dorrit Bern, in an interview in the late 1990s, Lane Bryant's customers are fierce loyalists who feel that the company knows exactly what they want and is an advocate for them.[8]

Because of demand shifting toward experiences, the new rules of retail are being led by those who want to blur the distinction between a material purchase and an experiential purchase. For instance, consumers are no longer satisfied with buying pants or jeans off a shelf, an item they don't need one more of. They will, however, seek the sensual, clublike experience of shopping in Abercrombie & Fitch, the young men's and women's casual sportswear chain. This experience starts with a roped-off entrance, complete with a bouncer, and includes a low-lit interior, loud rock music, sexy posters, alluring fragrance scents wafting throughout and sexily clad sales associates. Or consider Tommy Bahama's laid-back island resort store, which sells higher-priced casual wear for men and women, and where the layout opens onto a restaurant and bar, with live music playing throughout. Consumers will spend twice as much time enjoying the experience and will pay twice as much for a complete outfit than they would have in a traditional store—or, in the best-case scenario for the retailer, the experience itself might compel them to buy "just one more." It's the difference between buying lingerie off a rack in a department store and buying the experience provided by a Victoria's Secret, or between buying Barbie dolls or teddy bears in toy stores and creating your own, complete with names, birthdays— essentially an entire life story—in the festive, fun-filled workshops of the American Girl and Build-A-Bear stores. It's the move from plain old sporting goods stores to Cabela's, which offers free fly-fishing lessons, two-story mountains, waterfalls, trout ponds, etc. It's the difference between buying Maxwell House in a can and the Starbucks experience.

Other sectors have their own experiential standouts. They include the great shopping experiences at the new Apple computer stores, the flash sales on eBay and Zappos.com, all of which set the standard for emotionally connecting service. There are also the fresh, fun, food emporiums Whole Foods and Trader

Joe's, supermarkets unlike any other. The future of retailing is also foreshadowed by the growing propensity among consumers to move away from shopping in big stores, preferring instead the cozy experience and differentiated products in the growing number of independently owned neighborhood boutiques, like Junkman's Daughter in Atlanta, Georgia, which sells wigs, vintage apparel and costumes, all in a glittery, offbeat and wildly designed environment.

It's not just in the specialty retail brands or the independent mom-and-pop stores, though, that consumers expect an elevated experience. They expect every major retailer, from Wal-Mart to Neiman Marcus, from Home Depot to Best Buy, from McDonald's to the Outback Steakhouse, to provide a pleasant experience. Disney's retail component is repositioning all its stores to focus on elevating the shopping experience. From games to entertaining events to robust audiovisual presentations, it's all aimed at creating an emotionally connecting experience. Starbucks' recent unraveling was largely the result of losing its focus on experience, which was the core driver of its exponential growth, for the sake of cutting costs and pursuing an accelerated global growth strategy that was more efficiently executed with fewer experiential amenities. It is now desperately attempting to reinstate the experience. More and more traditional retailers are following suit. Of Bloomingdale's recently opened store in Dubai, their CEO, Michael Gould, was quoted in *Women's Wear Daily* as saying, "It's all about selling the experience."[9]

It's also important to note that the experiences anticipated or expected by consumers will vary according to the retailer, brand or service. For example, it is most likely a utilitarian or rational experience that the consumer expects from Wal-Mart or Dunkin' Donuts. Kohl's rapid growth was largely due to its business model's being totally organized around making the shopping experience convenient, easy and quick for the time-starved mom. Thus the experience is very utilitarian, but exactly what meets its consumers' expectations.

Consumers are also expecting some level of emotional experience from *wholesale* consumer brands and services of all types, simply because they can. This is driving wholesale brands such as The North Face, Juicy Couture, Nautica, Ralph Lauren, Apple, Microsoft, some P&G brands and others to roll out their own stores so they can better provide these experiences. They get to their consumers directly and more quickly, and because they own and control the point-of-sale, they control the presentation and the whole brand experience, from imaging to music to events—essentially the brand's entire DNA. This is an enormous and sustainable competitive advantage when compared with being jammed into a departmentalized retail environment, where the retailer will have cherry-picked items from the brand's line and presented it to consumers stuffed on racks and shelves.

The same holds true online. As stated by Ben Fischman, the CEO of online retailer Rue La La at a Macy's/Wharton Business School seminar in early 2010: "The first mistake of e-commerce is that we believed it was all about convenience."[10] His goal was to make their site fun, engaging, informational, exciting—an experience.

To take that point further, we believe online retailers such as Amazon, eBay and others will ultimately open brick-and-mortar, showroom-like stores, to be able to better create experiences for their more "touchy-feely" merchandise, such as apparel, for which creating an experience online is very difficult. Unlike traditional stores, these showrooms would be fun and engaging learning centers, and would have screens next to displayed merchandise to order for home delivery or pickup. Furthermore, such live showrooms would provide the human interaction and real-time consumer research not well facilitated online. Finally, thanks to the huge databases of these online retailers, they would be able to customize and localize their offerings and experiences according to consumer preferences almost by neighborhood.

To reiterate an important point: Consumers do not need "stuff" anymore. There's too much of it, all equally compelling. So all consumer-facing industries, whether retail, wholesale or services, must be able to understand and figure out how to deliver some kind of emotionally connecting experience.

From Conformity to Customization

Consumers are moving away from desiring mass-marketed mega-brands, meant to be a shared identity with fellow consumers. During Waves I and II, when there were fewer brands to select from, these national brands were considered cool. Consumers felt they were part of the in crowd if they wore the same logo as their friends and peer groups. Consumers still want what's cool, but cool is now according to their own definition. Today, as new brands proliferate on a daily basis, targeting specific consumer niches, consumers are shunning the need to be included, and are instead pursuing exclusivity. Another catalyst for this shift, of course, is easy access to information and knowledge about all products and services. So consumers now want something special, even customized, for their own particular desires, real or perceived.

In fact, brands like the Gap and Starbucks, which originally grew quickly in response to seemingly limitless markets, discovered that ubiquity (a store on every corner) became a major factor in their decline and they needed to reposition themselves. As consumers seek exclusivity, the brand that's available to anybody can quickly become uncool to everybody. Leading fashion-trend forecaster David Wolfe, of the Doneger Group, describes the new consumer landscape this way: "It's bye-bye mainstream and hello to thousands of tiny consumer tribes."[11]

These tiny niche tribes, in pursuit of special, exclusive value, are driving major changes in all consumer-facing businesses. The structure of the marketplace will be redefined as an infinite number of finite market segments ("communities") being served by an infinite number of finite brands, micromarketed through mediums that specifically target those niches.

Many branded-apparel specialty retailers understand this consumer shift. Accordingly, they are spinning off segmented niche brands, growing their original brand by extending it into other product and consumer markets. Examples include J. Crew, the men's and women's casual wear retailer, spinning off kids wear stores called CrewCuts, as well as a new line called Madewell, casual wear for the boomer market. Urban Outfitters, Free People and Anthropologie are all retail brands of URBN Inc. Each targets a different consumer segment, providing an eclectic mix of apparel and selected hard goods. Charming Shoppes, Inc., has three branded sportswear chains for different demographic niches of large-sized women: Fashion Bug, Catherine's, and Lane Bryant, as well as Cacique, a large-size intimate apparel store. Chico's, the casual-wear chain for boomer women, spun off the White House Black Market casual- and dress-wear stores for a younger consumer, and Soma, an intimate-apparel retail brand for boomers.

The shift toward exclusive niches also favors lifestyle brands such as Ralph Lauren, which is not linked to a single product or classification of products, or to one consumer segment. The brand can therefore launch into any consumer or product segment that is compatible with its brand positioning of Ralph Lauren as an upscale, elegant and sophisticated style of living. The brands that were launched and heavily marketed as single-product mega-brands, such as Levi's Jeans, have found it extremely difficult, if not impossible, to launch their names in other product or consumer markets. Furthermore, consumers, with their closets overstuffed with all kinds of brands, will tend to try a brand that isn't being worn by everybody else, rather than choosing yet another one of the ubiquitous mega-brands. After all, in 1980, they had a choice of about six major blue jean brands. Today there are hundreds.

Traditional department stores are also being forced to meet the expectations of the exclusivity-seeking consumer. They are forging exclusivity agreements with designers and national wholesale brands as well as accelerating their private branding programs. In a recent study, NPD, the primary retail industry source for consumer sales information, found that in 1975, 25 percent of all apparel consisted of private or exclusive brands. That number reached close to 50 percent in 2005, and NPD predicted it would reach 60 percent by 2010.[12] Macy's has exclusivity agreements with Tommy Hilfiger, Martha Stewart and others, as well as private brands INC, Alfani and more. It also has a localization program called "My Macy's," which distributes different line mixes to different stores based on geographically variant consumer preferences, as does Best Buy. It's estimated that private and exclusive brands make up over 50 percent of JCPenney's revenues. Five of its private brands, including Arizona, Stafford and St. John's Bay, each provide over a billion dollars in revenue per year. JCPenney's exclusives include Liz Claiborne, Sephora, Mango, Nicole Miller and many more. Moreover, Kohl's, Target and even Wal-Mart continue to accelerate their private and exclusive branding strategies.

In grocery stores across the United States, the penetration of private brands has reached 15 percent of total sales, and is continuing to accelerate. Recent studies found that close to 80 percent of consumers across all income strata said that store brands are as good, if not better, than national brands.[13] Such consumer preference will continue to drive the growth of private branding. A good example is Whole Foods, where growth of private brands was four times the rate of national brands during the recession, ca. 2007–2010, and even now it continues two and half times faster. There is still a big gap on this front between the United States and Europe, where 60 percent of grocery store brands are private. But consumer choices will close the gap in the United States.

The huge growth of small, independently owned retail boutiques can largely be attributed to consumers' pursuit of special products and services. The National Retail Federation recently conducted a study that found the fastest-growing retail sector across all consumer segments and price points is that of the small stores.

In fact, they made up over half of the one hundred fastest-growing stores in 2006.

Finally, there are many brands and retailers, both online and through catalogs and stores, that can provide actual custom-made products. One example is the Nike/Hurley/Converse combo store that offers in-store product customization. Each consumer can select from a series of designs and color schemes to personalize shirts or shoes. While shoppers wait for their customized products, the store offers an experience: an environment where people can listen to music, lounge about with friends and just hang out. Vans sneakers provides a similar customization service online.

Another factor favoring smaller, segmented niche brands is the fact that in slow-growing markets, brands reach maturity more quickly than in underserved, fast-growing markets such as in Wave II. Their life cycles are much shorter. They cannot grow infinitely; they must steal a limited share of market with one brand. Paradoxically, the more niche brands there are, the more they benefit, because they're all taking share from the mega-brands. And the consumer will make sure that this axiom continues indefinitely as their quest for "something special for me" continues to gain momentum.

Barry Schwartz's *The Paradox of Choice: Why More is Less* also describes the consumer shift that now seeks exclusivity and "special for me" products and services. Being overwhelmed by piles of stuff in a poorly edited store is a bad experience. However, 800 blue jean brands, with each one positioned and tailored for a specific consumer niche, is totally consistent with the thesis that "less is more," and also very close to customized.

From Plutocracy to Democracy

Armed with their newfound wealth and on their search for happiness, consumers have shifted from accepting the notion that only the wealthy deserve luxury to demanding "democracy"—affordable luxury for all classes. This shift helped create a new consumer segment, "luxury aspirants," and drove the launch of many brands to cater to the up-market "yuppie" core of that segment. Brands such as Coach, Lacoste, Bloomingdale's, Cusp (a Neiman Marcus spin-off), Dooney & Burke, Tory Burch and others have successfully captured the contemporary, young, not-quite-rich but well-off luxury consumer.

Further down-market, the democratization of luxury is being catered to by designers creating brands for mainstream retailers. For example, Mossimo, Michael Graves, Jean Paul Gaultier and others have designed discount lines for Target; Norma Kamali can be found at Wal-Mart; Vera Wang at Kohl's; Nicole Miller at JCPenney; and Marc Jacobs, Stella McCartney, and others at Macy's. This evolution is the result of the same market forces driving the other shifts. Luxury-level designers and brands found it increasingly difficult to achieve adequate and profitable growth in over-competed, slow-growing markets. Therefore, *diffusion,* in the form of sub-brands like those cited, continues in all channels of distribution. Concurrently, on the demand side, consumers' expectations continue to rise to the level of the selection they are given, thereby perpetually raising the bar for the supply side. And this in turn will perpetuate the democratization of the marketplace.

Finally, as consumers have become more knowledgeable through access to greater amounts of information, they are better able to understand the true value of the products and services they are shopping for. Mobile electronic devices, or online searches, can compare prices in a matter of seconds. Therefore, consumers are much more closely scrutinizing price/value relationships. Consumers' blind acceptance of any price tag on a luxury item, just to be able to flaunt the name among their wealthy peer groups, is giving way to their demand for real value. This reassessment of value has led to selective quality trumping quantity and "bling." As Burt

Tansky, CEO of Neiman Marcus said: "Our wealthy customers used to buy a designer bag without even looking at the price tag. Today, they are comparing the bag to the price, and there is nobody who understands value better than our customers."

From New to New *and* Now

New no longer trumps all. Consumers still want new, but they also expect to have it right here, right now. Innovation itself is not enough to win in a 24/7 world, where what's created today is cloned tomorrow. It's now necessary to create knock offs of *yourself* every day of the week.

The reasons we desire new, fresh and frequent products everywhere is rooted, once again, in our desire for happiness. Recent studies have shown that when consumers go shopping and discover something new, the brain releases dopamine and serotonin (chemicals associated with feelings of well-being, satisfaction, happiness, contentment and addiction). As Dr. David Lewis, the director of Mindlab International, has said: "Shopping experiences trigger brain activity that creates these 'euphoric moments.' But what is most interesting is that these 'euphoric moments' can be created by the frequency of new items in the stores and the expectation of finding something unexpected."[14] A *Wall Street Journal* article reported on a study of rats that found "when a rat explored a new place, dopamine surged in its brain's reward center."[15] This would certainly be the equivalent to a consumer discovering a new store, mall, brand, or even a new store assortment and layout.

Additionally, a research team from Emory University found that dripping Kool-Aid into the mouths of volunteers on a regular basis had little increase in brain activity, while those who were given random "dripping" had a heightened level of activity. This indicates that the anticipation of the reward, whether it is Kool-Aid or a new dress, is what gets consumers' dopamine pumping. Retailers are starting to use these neuroscientific insights to gain share by providing "new and now" value, along with experiences, of course.

A good example of the shift to "new and now" is Zara, the Spain-based apparel chain with over two thousand stores around the world. Zara has proven that supply-chain innovation trumps product innovation, by delivering two new lines every week to each of its stores, meaning the line mix may be different for two different stores just a few blocks apart, based on the consumer preferences of each. Zara's average core consumer annual visitation rate is seventeen, compared to a retail industry average of about four, simply because Zara fans are compelled to see the twice-weekly new lines. They are also compelled to buy something if they like it, knowing it might not be there the following week. H&M and Forever 21 are also a part of the "fast fashion" club, and others are racing to adopt this model.

Not confined to fast fashion, Costco has its own version of new and now. It has a "treasure hunt" component in the middle of the store to offer a new and now experience with interesting, selective and often not-repeated merchandise. People go to the store with dopamine already surging in anticipation of what they might find. Trader Joe's does the same thing by often changing and replacing high-selling items. The Gilt Groupe online membership club utilizes the same principle. It offers new and exclusive luxury merchandise in the form of membership-only sales every thirty-six hours, which keeps the dopamine surging and members rushing to their computers every day so as not to miss the sales.

From Self to Community

Finally, one of the more positive results of accessible abundance is that many consumers are now able to achieve the pinnacle of Maslow's hierarchy of needs: self-actualization. Their material desires are being satisfied and they are able to move toward maximizing their human potential: to seek knowledge, peace, aesthetic experiences and so forth. Logically, this shift includes heightened interest in community over self. One major manifestation of this shift, as well as one of its ongoing enablers, is the phenomenal growth of electronic social networks. While these rapidly populating worldwide "communities" are the commercial targets of many retailers and consumer product companies, they are finding that traditional marketing pushes fail. They must be given permission to enter these communities, and they are not allowed to sell in the classic way. Businesses must shift from talking *to*, or talking *at*, to conversing *with* the consumer. The various new retail clubs on the Internet such as Gilt Groupe, Rue La La, Net-A-Porter and many others are communities within themselves, attracting millions of consumers. There are also plenty of ways to create a community environment offline and add brand authenticity, such as what many health and fitness stores (lululemon, for example) are doing: offering classes and links to trainers and local events, all of which makes members feel part of a broader community.

This shift toward self-actualization has an altruistic element to it as well. The consumption binge of the last quarter-century reached epic proportions, and then crashed early in the new millennium. This experience fed into the realization among consumers that self-actualization should take the form of "less is more," even among the wealthy. In correlation to the shift from plutocracy to democracy described above, ostentation has given way to understatement.

Furthermore, consumers are finding satisfaction in taking up causes, such as environmental advocacy and charity work. The remarkable strength of this trend is driving businesses to attach their commercial efforts to these same causes. Wal-Mart is a great example of leading "sustainability" initiatives in the retail and consumer product industries: reducing the toxic emissions of their huge trucking fleet; selling only fluorescent light bulbs; forcing its vendors to reduce the volume of their packaging; and much more. The day after the devastating earthquake in Haiti in 2010, the high-end online fashion club Rue La La suspended its daily online sale and instead directed its members to the Red Cross website, suggesting they divert their planned Rue La La spending to the Haiti cause. The subsequent member accolades and increased spending were enormous.

On the other hand, the giant Nestlé was blindsided by environmental activists using social media to attack them for their purchases of palm oil, which they use in Kit Kat candy bars. As reported in the March 29, 2010 issue of the *Wall Street Journal*, protesters have posted a negative video on YouTube, deluged Nestlé's Facebook page and peppered Twitter with claims that Nestlé is contributing to the destruction of Indonesia's rain forest, potentially exacerbating global warming and endangering orangutans.[16] The allegations stem from Nestlé's purchases of palm oil from an Indonesian company that Greenpeace International says has cleared rain forest to establish palm plantations. So, just as those who do the *right* environmental thing will attract and even convert consumers, those who don't are at great risk of losing business or even being publicly shamed, particularly by younger consumer cohorts.

The winning businesses of the future will understand and respond to these five major consumer shifts. And by turning their brands into compelling communities that generate ideas, causes and/or other altruistic concepts, as opposed to just selling stuff, they will succeed.

A Final Cultural Shift?

In many ways, all these shifting consumer desires may portend a cultural shift away from the characteristics of our age. Following is a quick snapshot of the five major consumer shifts driving the seven major strategic and structural shifts from Waves II to III.

This chart also simply diagrams the logic we used to develop our thesis, depicting the combined shifts driving the three imperative strategic operating principles necessary for success in the twenty-first century.

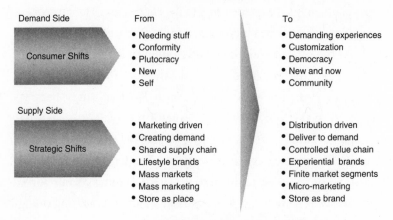

Consumer Market Shifts

Demand Side

Consumer Shifts

From	To
• Needing stuff	• Demanding experiences
• Conformity	• Customization
• Plutocracy	• Democracy
• New	• New and now
• Self	• Community

Supply Side

Strategic Shifts

• Marketing driven	• Distribution driven
• Creating demand	• Deliver to demand
• Shared supply chain	• Controlled value chain
• Lifestyle brands	• Experiential brands
• Mass markets	• Finite market segments
• Mass marketing	• Micro-marketing
• Store as place	• Store as brand

Imperative strategic operating principles
- • Neurological connectivity
- • Preemptive distribution
- • Value chain control

Figure 4.2: Consumer market shifts

PART 2

THE NEW
RULES OF RETAIL

CHAPTER 5

MAKING THE
MIND CONNECTION

NEUROLOGICAL CONNECTIVITY

As we have pointed out in earlier chapters, there are new rules of consumer connectivity. It is no longer about the physical connection of products or services with consumers. This, too, is simply a point of entry. Far more important is the "mind" connection, or what we define as neurological connectivity. If there is one common success factor that runs through all five consumer value shifts cited in chapter 4, it's that in order to fulfill consumer demands, a retailer or brand or service must first determine how to make its particular value offering so powerfully satisfying that it actually changes the consumer's brain chemistry. The requirement is that it must be so mentally and emotionally compelling that at the mere mention of the brand or retailer or service, the consumer's brain releases a shot of dopamine, which triggers an instant desire to get or go to that brand. For those of us who have eaten at In-N-Out Burger, shopped at lululemon or wanted to see what Target's $1 spot has on offer, the concept is readily understood.

It is vital to understand the distinction between neurological connectivity and traditional brand management. The concepts are overlapping—of course brands have always sought positive mental reactions from their consumers—but far from synonymous. A simple example explains the differences. Zara, the apparel retail specialty chain, has developed its brand based on some highly specific and pragmatic consumer benefits, which their customers can readily identify and describe. They would explain that Zara has fresh new assortments almost every week, that its prices are below competitors' and that it has a nice broad range of products: apparel, accessories, shoes and bags. And even though Zara built the brand with minimal advertising (0.3 percent of revenues versus 3–4 percent for most traditional brand advertisers and their competitors), it is widely known among its target consumers for its unique brand attributes.

However, what consumers will not articulate is that Zara has developed a neurological connection with them. In fact, the term does not exist in most consumers' vocabulary. It's also unlikely that Zara's management would refer to this great competitive advantage as a neurological connection. But in fact it is. It has created an experience that triggers a dopamine surge in the consumer's brain. This occurs around the regularly scheduled deliveries of new, select and limited-time merchandise. To put it simply, Zara has a brand with "a sense of tantalizing exclusivity."[1] This would not be the case if it employed traditional brand management, however competently.

Neuroscientists have proven that the anticipation of rewards—or the potential of *not* getting what you want—will produce dopamine, which actively drives behavior. As we pointed out, this is why consumers visit Zara seventeen times per year, compared to three to four for traditional retailers, because they are afraid of missing something new and exciting. It also compels them to buy in fear of the item's being bought by someone else. Zara's whole business model is built around this goal. The online retailer Gilt Groupe does the same with its select, limited-time offerings that consumers anxiously await. These elements are part and parcel of the brand, but transcend the traditional elements of brand positioning and equity: brand awareness, perceived quality, associations and conscious loyalty.

We believe neurological connectivity is achieved when a retailer, brand or service creates a strong psychological and physical response that operates on a subconscious level for the consumer and that is typically not readily understood or necessarily recognized by the consumer. Simply stated, a brand or store has a neurological connection with customers if they approach the store visit as they would a visit to the home of a good friend. The trip requires almost no perceivable effort because they know it is going to be a fun and enjoyable experience.

And, lest you think that *neuroconnectivity* is just another marketing buzzword, new research methodologies and studies have discovered and confirmed this powerful connecting dynamic between products, services and consumers. Two recent examples capture the importance that consumer package companies place on trying to establish this connection.

> The Hershey Co. is spending a lot of time in grocery and other retail stores these days to get inside customers' heads. CEO David J. West is so sold on this kind of grocery aisle consumer research that he told a conference of food analysts that the results would give Hershey a "competitive advantage in our category for years to come." Already, Hershey has psychological profiles on its array of customers. For these shoppers to splurge, almost everything has to be perfect—price, packaging, product display—or they'll zoom past without adding any Hershey's candy to their grocery carts. After four straight years of increasing advertising spending, which should top $300 million this year, Hershey is putting its marketing money where consumers spend theirs: in the grocery and retail outlets where its candy is sold in the aisles and at the registers.[2]

Later we will also explain why the dollars spent on traditional media (advertising) are becoming less effective and why they are better spent on understanding and driving the in-store experience.

Consider another example: For two years, Campbell's researchers studied microscopic changes in skin moisture, heart rate and other biometrics to see how consumers react to everything from pictures of bowls of soup to logo design. According to a February 17, 2010, article in the *Wall Street Journal*, "This 'neuromarketing' approach is a fresh attempt by companies to better understand how consumers respond. . . . The Campbell's team figured it could boost sales by triggering more emotional responses in stores and prompting more people to focus on more soups."[3]

All these reports reinforce the power of this subconscious mind connection. And while we are still in the early stages of understanding of how this process works, the evidence suggests that subtle neural processes are a powerful driver of our shopping behaviors.[4] Our goal in this chapter is to connect this research to the winning business models of Wave III.

So how do we think it works? The business model is designed to drive the entire experience of three things: the dopamine rush in anticipation of shopping, compelling the consumer to visit the store; the ecstasy of the actual shopping experience itself; and the final satisfaction of consuming or using the product or service. This is the neurological connection with the consumer on all conscious and subconscious levels.

When successfully executed, these experiences are co-created by the consumer, and retailer, brand or service. The experience may be set up, or provided by, the Container Store, for example, but the consumer "shapes" or creates the experience to satisfy his or her personal desire at the very moment they are in the store. The "set up" is Container Store's highly trained associates (up to 235 hours of training vs. 7 to 8 for traditional retailers), who act more as consultants than sales people. They spend as much time as necessary to discuss with and advise each customer on their specific storage needs. The co-created experience, therefore, is shaped by the customer's individual situation and the satisfaction of having a real expert solve their unique problem. This co-creation of a neurological experience is indelible, unique and immeasurable.

And because the experience is co-created at one moment in time, a completely new and unique experience will be co-created the next time the consumer visits the Container Store, which adds to the force of the neurological connection. One might then suggest that this dynamic will increase the brain's reaction even upon merely hearing the name of the store. To be sure, one cannot attach a quantitative value to a neurological experience, since it will be different each time. It is for this reason that control of that experience is so critical.

We can borrow from the language of academia to elaborate on this point: "Value creation is defined by the experience of a specific consumer, at a specific point in time and location, in the context of a specific event. The experience space is conceptually distinct from that of the product space, which is the conventional focus of innovation. In the experience space, the individual consumer is central, and an event triggers a co-creation experience. The events have a context in space and time, and the involvement of the individual influences that experience. The personal meaning derived from the co-creation experience is what determines the value to the individual."[5] In other words, each time one visits a friend, one has a uniquely enjoyable time that cannot be repeated outside of that relationship.

So, providing a wonderful new product or brand that has great functionality, awareness and high overall value (and even generates an emotional connection) may get you to the retail "playoffs," but, as we have said, to win the championship you must make a neurological connection.

Creating Connectivity

So how does one create neurological connectivity? The retailer, brand or service must align its brand positioning to deliver one or more of any of the five consumer value shifts, and then it must create those elements that will neurologically connect with the consumer. And it's important to emphasize that this process of creating the connection must be an integral part of one's business model, culturally, financially and relative to the entire value chain. This must not be viewed as a simply peripheral "add-on" to the business. If so, the process will fail.

In researching this process, we came upon some studies from *Scientific American* on why people fall in love, which is perhaps one of our most powerful experiences.[6] Following are some principles in the studies that we think could translate to equivalent neurological retail experiences:

Creating Arousal

Research suggests that people bond emotionally when they are aroused (e.g., through exercise, smell or when challenged). So lululemon puts exercise classes in its stores; Starwood Hotels and Abercrombie & Fitch place perfume in certain locations; and, of course, the smell of coffee in Starbucks is a familiar neuroconnector. The challenge of the "treasure hunt" in Costco is a part of that brand's DNA. And Gilt Groupe's daily, narrowly timed luxury sales have their customers anxiously waiting at the starting gate. On a more obvious level, the semiclad associates at A&F stores are designed to create arousal, because people spend more and are less inhibited when aroused.

Proximity and Familiarity

Research conducted at Stanford University suggests that simply being around people provokes positive feelings. Best Buy, Bloomingdale's and other retailers' small-store neighborhood strategies seek such proximity (see the discussion of preemptive distribution in the next chapter), and it establishes them more as familiar "neighbors" than just a store. This also reinforces the value of having traffic drivers to the store and an operating model of "resets"—new merchandise that continually drives the consumer to return.

Similarity

Additional research from MIT proves that people seek others with similar interests and lifestyles. So word of mouth and the use of social networking continue to flourish as neurologically connecting strategies. JCPenney had an incredible viral hit with its YouTube video during the 2009 holidays. Several husbands are in the "doghouse"—literally, in a constructed look-alike. Each has to go before an all-female review board while their wives are also present to seek release, having to answer, for example, as to why he bought his wife a vacuum cleaner for her anniversary present, or why another stayed out on Christmas Eve playing poker, etc. As they give their excuses, the judge stamps "denied" on all but the poker guy, who's pulled a necklace out of his pocket to make it up to his wife. The socially networked people passed this video around to their communities and JCPenney's became a part of the in crowd.

Novelty

This is one of the key elements of the consumer value shift to the new and now, as discussed in chapter 4. As we mentioned previously, Zara, the Spain-based global retail chain, delivers two new lines every week to over two thousand stores, thus compelling consumers to visit more often. The online luxury membership club Gilt Groupe has exclusive sales of totally new merchandise every thirty-six hours, encouraging members to visit every day. Wal-Mart, in its "clean up the store" initiative, increased the frequency of store resets. And Anthropologie has different layouts in each of the stores in its chain. These strategies, while creating novel and frequent experiences, are of course also complex to implement.

Kindness, Accommodation and Forgiveness

This kind of human behavior can be paralleled by neuroconnecting levels of service at such retailers as Nordstrom's, Mitchells in Greenwich, Connecticut, Zappos, Apple, Best Buy and others.

Touch and Sexuality

All one has to do is visit an A&F store in order to have four of the five senses bombarded with the sexuality of sight, sound, smell and touch. Others might equally connect to the Victoria's Secret experience.

Self-Disclosure

Other evidence proves that people bond when they share a secret, providing a sense of vulnerability. For example, one of the reasons Wal-Mart's pharmacy is so successful is that customers feel they have shared a well-kept secret, and that Wal-Mart is looking after them. Some experts contend that customers who use the pharmacy spend more money and time in the store than their counterparts who do not use the pharmacy.

Commitment

Finally, research from Purdue University suggests that commitment is critical for love.[7] Chico's meteoric rise through the 1990s can largely be attributed to its commitment to the female boomer segment, just as committed advocacy for the plus-size consumer proved successful for Lane Bryant, Fashion Bug and Catherine's. In essence those retailers are saying, "We're here for you—and only you!"

While creating the neurological connection is imperative for achieving success, it's essential that the connecting experience is

tightly and credibly aligned with the brand's or retailer's positioning, or DNA, in a way that consumers find believable, natural and
compelling. Failure to do so not only is deleterious to the brand,
but it can actually put the business at risk. As exemplified in the article "Making Routine Customer Experiences Fun" in the MIT
Sloan Management Review:

> Changing a neutral experience into a positive one isn't easy, and
> there's no guarantee of success for companies that make the at-
> tempt. In the early 1990s, Tandy Corp. failed to get traction with
> its Incredible Universe superstores. The stores featured music,
> karaoke, laser shows and door prizes. The company carefully se-
> lected and trained employees and emulated Disney's approach
> to interactions between staff and customers. But after 17 super-
> stores had been built, Tandy pulled the plug on these money-los-
> ing ventures. The fun elements weren't enough to make the stores
> profitable in the competitive consumer-electronics segment.[8]

Finally, there is an emerging trend that is perhaps one of the
most powerful of all mind influencers and neuroconnectivity: virtual reality. While this trend is still in its infancy, the U.S. Army is
a great example of its potential power. In Philadelphia, the army
has closed four of its traditional recruiting centers and opened a
new Army Experience Center.[9] "Hands-on virtual reality experiences and simulations allow users to see, touch and learn firsthand
what it means to be in the Army." As one seventeen-year-old remarked: "It's fun. It gives you the real experience. You can hang
out and play games with your friends."[10] With over fourteen thousand visitors in just fifteen months, its traffic-building power has
already been proven. Whether it will help with gaining recruits is
still in question. The larger message, however, is that given the
widespread addiction to virtual-reality games on the web, the influence is likely to be immense. It is only a matter of time before
leading retailers begin to use these technologies to further connect
neurologically with their consumers.

As we conclude our discussion of neurological connectivity,
we should remember that this connection precedes, but does not

preclude, its essential partner—preemptive distribution, another of the three imperative strategic operating shifts. In fact, as we just pointed out, the neurological connection is itself the most powerful preemptive distribution strategy, because once the connection is made, the brand is indelibly first and foremost in the consumer's mind, compelling them to get or go to that brand first, and to go back to it again, before they go anywhere else: read, to a competitor.

In the next chapter, we will discuss how to capitalize on that victory.

CHAPTER 6

REDEFINING THE RULES OF ENGAGEMENT

PREEMPTIVE DISTRIBUTION

Another consumer-driven paradigm shift severely challenges the distribution strategies of Waves I and II, relegating them to entry-level status. Technology and globalization have accelerated the growth of new distribution platforms, most notably the Internet, which has intensified the already hypercompetitive environment. The shift, as discussed earlier, is from the store as the locus of activity—when everyone would "go to the store"—to consumers as the locus, requiring the store to come to them, literally and figuratively. Consumers expect total access, because they can. Access whenever, wherever and however they desire it is the new normal.

During Waves I and II, we evolved from general stores in the center of town to bigger stores and chains, still centrally located in malls and shopping centers. Retailers could say, "Build it and they will come," and they did. In Wave III consumers say, "Deliver it to me," and retailers must.

For those brick-and-mortar stores that wish to remain in the center, the only exceptions to this new normal will be those that have achieved neurological connectivity so powerfully compelling that consumers are willing to go back to the brick-and-mortar location for the experience.

Furthermore, while consumers are in the center, they are not static. They are constantly moving targets. This alone is forcing businesses to elevate their level of distribution expertise. Finally— in a change that has enormous implications for the marketing, advertising and media industries—those businesses cannot just "push" their offerings onto consumers. They must be invited or given permission. And as advertising loses some of its credibility with increasingly savvy consumers, word of mouth is driving more sales. Marketers in consumer-facing industries can no longer talk at their targets. They must *engage* with them, often through their trusted friends and colleagues. In fact, in marketing lingo, "communities" are the new segments. Consumers and their desires can no longer be accurately identified by lumping them together in big, demographically defined groups. The market can now be described as an infinite number of finite consumer segments, or thousands of tiny consumer "tribes."

All these shifts in consumers' desires and accessibility mean that retailers and brands must innovate new ways to gain access to these consumers, leading us to identify and define another imperative strategic operating principle: preemptive distribution.

Preemptive Distribution

What is preemptive distribution? First of all, it's an attempt to address the overcompeted marketplace. It responds to the fact that consumers have hundreds of equally compelling choices, literally right at their fingertips, across the street or knocking on their front door. So it's understood that the competitor that gets to the consumer first, quicker and most often, preempting the hundreds of others, has a better chance of winning share. The strategy also requires distribution precisely where, when and how the consumer wishes to receive it. By definition, then, preemptive distribution requires an integrated matrix of all relevant distribution mediums, including distribution into faster-growing international markets.

However, there are three other important elements of this strategic imperative that we must also examine:

1. Preemptive distribution does not equal ubiquitous distribution, nor does it mean every retailer must open more stores. It must be precisely aligned with where, when, how and how often the consumers want to receive the product or service. And today the distribution must be unobtrusive. Some experts believe a large part of the Gap's and Starbucks' setbacks was due to their ubiquity (a store on every corner) and their cost cutting to achieve scale, both of which ultimately resulted in a "sameness" and consumer boredom. Furthermore, the new consumers hate to be intruded upon. They will invite or give permission to those brands they want in their lives, and when and how they want them. Ubiquitous and intrusive marketing and distribution will drive them away.

2. Preemptive distribution does not mean that all consumer-facing businesses must be on all distribution platforms. Some are simply not relevant for all business models. One way to measure the viability of a given distribution platform is the degree to which it reinforces or enables the attainment of the five "shifted" consumer desires. For example, why should the Gilt Groupe's members' club on the Internet ever open a brick-and-mortar store? It delivers on all five consumer desires: it provides a neurologically connecting experience (the consumer can't wait to key into the one-hour daily sale of discounted luxury goods); its sale for "members only" gives the perception of scarcity and special customization, as well as af-

fordable luxury; it delivers on "new and now" by showcasing all new products every day; it creates a sense of urgency because the product will not be back; and finally, it's certainly a "community." On the other hand, Amazon, with its huge databases of consumer knowledge (who and where they are, and what they want), could easily justify a preemptive brick-and-mortar strategy for their fashion, beauty and footwear businesses, which would answer the customer need for feel and fit required in those categories. In showroom-like stores they could showcase only the products that the locals desire, as mined from their data, and create a neuroexperience by using new technology that allows consumers to customize outfits that can then be ordered online, in the store and delivered to their homes. Somewhat counterintuitively, TV retailers HSN and QVC do, in fact, have brick-and-mortar stores: HSN has about twenty-five, in which it sells home and apparel lifestyle brands; and QVC has a few showcase stores and several outlet stores.

3. Preemptive distribution is not just *physically* preemptive. As we just pointed out, neurologically connected brands are the most powerful "preemptors." They preempt the competition before the consumer even taps into a site or goes to a store, by triggering the dopamine rush. Ironically, one of the ultimate effects of achieving this connection may actually be a reduction in stores, thereby increasing productivity. If the connection is strong enough, as in yoga chain lululemon, a customer will bypass a competing store that might be right across the street to get to his or her lululemon "fix" a mile away.

From "Silos" to Integration to Preemption

Distribution in the faster-growing marketplaces of Waves I and II was fairly simple and straightforward. As stated, retailers opened stores and consumers came shopping. There was not yet too much competition. And, even as competition accelerated in Wave II, along with an increase in distribution platforms, retailers and wholesalers alike operated their distribution strategies vertically, in "silos." For example, Sears' or JCPenney's catalog operations were organized and run separately from their store operations. Most wholesale brands, like Levi's Jeans, Tide soap and Coca-Cola had not even begun to think about owning or controlling their distribution, nor were there the myriad of distribution platforms that have expanded into Wave III, including TV, direct mail, catalogs, door-to-door selling, in-home marketing, event marketing, kiosks, airlines and trains, flea markets, street promotions, traveling van promotions and others. And no one had ever heard of the Internet.

The ratcheting up of consumer demands and competition has therefore prioritized the development of distribution strategies. Essentially, the winners will be managing an enormous matrix of distribution mediums, and they must all be carefully integrated so that the consumer can cross over easily from one to the other for different purposes: research, buying, returning and customer service, whether they are stationary or on the move. Furthermore, all consumer-facing businesses must determine which platforms are relevant to the value they are distributing, how they support a preemptive strategy and whether they can be smoothly integrated into the matrix.

Stores to Consumers

Preemptive distribution also means taking brick-and-mortar stores to the consumer, literally across the street in the neighborhoods where they live. Beyond the independently owned small retailers, many large mall and freestanding big-box retailers are spinning off smaller, freestanding stores placed in the consumers' neighborhoods, thus providing immediate, preemptive access.

Kohl's was arguably one of the first traditional department store retailers to launch this strategy in the early 1990s. Identifying its core consumer as the time-starved working mom, who did not have time to drive to and shop through the mall, Kohl's designed small, one-story, wide-aisled, quickly traversable stores, with central checkout and big parking lots. And they placed them in neighborhoods with lots of families.

Some experts have suggested that this preemptive distribution strategy is largely responsible for Kohl's explosive $10 billion growth during the 1990s, and that the majority of those revenues were stolen from JCPenney, because Kohl's core working-mom consumer had access right across the street to an equally compelling retail experience. JCPenney finally did acknowledge the loss of share due to Kohl's strategy, and subsequently developed and launched a smaller, freestanding, off-mall store strategy.

The same thing is happening now across the entire retail spectrum. Wal-Mart has a small-store format for urban and suburban neighborhoods, and is sensitive to the perils of being overly intrusive, designing its facades and landscaping to meld with the local environment. Best Buy has launched 3500–5000-square-foot neighborhood stores with different nameplates, preemptively distributing to different localized needs. Smaller-format dollar and convenience stores are rapidly expanding into local areas across the country. And, of course, the construction of smaller shopping villages within neighborhoods is on the increase, while regional malls are being shuttered or renovated to provide a better shopping experience: entertainment; restaurants; fashion shows; and so forth. The more rapidly growing, independently owned neighborhood boutiques, moreover, literally exemplify preemptive distribution, as well as a neurological connection to their very narrow consumer niches.

We predict that ultimately the continual pursuit of preemptive distribution will also drive the traditional department stores to spin off branded retail specialty chains, carrying their growing private and/or exclusive brands (i.e., Arizona stores for JCPenney, INC stores for Macy's and others).

Bring It to Me, Just for Me, New and More Often

Delivering on consumer expectations also means that the products or services desired must be accessible on the distribution platform of choice, precisely when consumers want it, even if they are mobile. In fact, mobile e-commerce is expected to enter a rapid growth trajectory, matching the double-digit rates of stationary Internet growth, according to many experts.

A great example of a company embracing the beginnings of digital retailing, so to speak, and embedding one's brand into social communities is Disney. They are connected to 33 million people in 130 Disney-sponsored Facebook sites. Disney's strategy is to engage consumers in a dialogue and an exchange of information. Disney has points of interest for the consumer and, accordingly, they can learn more about their consumers.

Facebook also has a partnership with Fandango, the online movie-ticket purchasing service, so that when a consumer buys a movie ticket through Fandango the consumer's Facebook friends are automatically notified and invited along. As Robert Iger, CEO of Disney said: "This kind of 'word-of-mouth' among friends about a movie or anything else for that matter, is worth seven times that of a recommendation from any other source. This new approach will destroy traditional media."[1]

Apple is another example of a brand talking "with" its consumers (vs. "at" them), and therefore gaining information about what interests them and what might compel them to keep revisiting its site. When a customer signs up for the Genius service on iTunes they give Apple permission to pull the data from their music and movie libraries. Armed with this information, Apple can not only determine what that customer likes, but also what friends and other consumers in the same cohort might like as well.

The future opportunities provided by this kind of mobile retailing and interconnectivity with consumer communities are enormous. Simply recommending purchases is quickly becoming the most basic use. The more advanced brands will be creating communities of their own in such a way that they will attract fans (that is, more loyal customers).

While e-commerce (including mobile), catalogs, direct mail and other mobility-serving distribution platforms are obvious for taking the product or service to the consumer, they do not preclude some of the strategies emerging from the more traditional distribution platforms. The winners in these sectors are pursuing the customization and localization of their stores, product mixes, presentations and services, all according to consumer preferences in different regions, cities and even neighborhoods. Best Buy's small neighborhood stores, mentioned above, are an example. Their "Escape" and "Super-D" stores have different store layouts, line mixes and service levels according to the preferences and needs of the local consumer base (for example, a retirement neighborhood may need more tech help than a yuppie locale).

The "My Macy's" program also distributes localized line mixes. Wrangler, a jeans and casual wear brand of VF Corporation, has the capability to deliver two different line mixes to two different doors of Wal-Mart that may be across town from each other. Wal-Mart is testing a "store of the community" strategy, which will customize every store format and merchandise for local preferences. And giant U.K. grocer Tesco has five specialized food formats, 7-Eleven-type convenience stores, and Tesco.com. It continues to expand its preemptive, localized model in the United States.

To successfully execute localization, the marketing end of the businesses must integrate qualitative and quantitative research; census, demographic and lifestyle data; sales tracking; loyalty cards; Internet sales; competitive intelligence; local management information; and even unsolicited comments, all from decentralized local stores and markets. All this information must also be continually fed into a highly centralized operations and distribution end of the business, to ensure that these large operations successfully distribute such decentralized, localized line mixes. Successful localization yields enormous increases in sales (up to 40 and 50 percent in some cases) and a reduction in inventory and markdowns.

Finally, customizing or localizing is very difficult for competitors to copy, therefore providing a more sustainable competitive advantage. It encourages and rewards innovation and differentiation and ultimately builds a brand personality that connects in a neurological and emotional way with local consumers. Conversely, mass homogenization impedes innovation and rewards tightly disciplined operational efficiencies, ultimately eliminating strategic differentiation and the growth and profitability that accompany it.

A preemptive distribution strategy also benefits from shorter product/service cycles by distributing more new lines more often. In the apparel industry, this is called "fast fashion." H&M, Uniqlo, Mango and Forever 21, along with previously mentioned Zara, all employ it.

The superior controlled and managed value chains of these brands are powerful examples of how process and systems' innovation can actually trump product innovation. It's easy to knock off a product, but not so easy to knock off a business model.

Even the traditional retailers and wholesalers are pushing their envelopes. Through better management and control of their value chains, also enabled by technology and globalization, they are reducing line cycles, thereby turning out more new lines more often.

Global Preemption

Consumer-facing industries in the mature U.S. marketplace can no longer ignore the necessity to gain a preemptive position in the developing countries that have much faster and sustainable growth rates. And it's not simply the need for growth that presses a sense of urgency. The world has become "flat," interconnected in so many ways that if brands and retailers fail to gain a preemptive presence globally, they will find their home-based positions severely weakened. This is due to the fact that consumers are globally mobile, literally and electronically, and therefore, they must be distributed to preemptively, wherever they are. Furthermore, the neuro-experience must also be consistent worldwide.

Adding urgency to preemptive global expansion is the fact that the infrastructures in many countries are still relatively fluid. As they begin to mature, the opportunities will decline, and in some countries may simply be gone.

The challenges of expanding internationally are many, and vary widely depending on the myriad political, economic, social, consumer and marketplace issues of the host country. An equal number of issues exist for the business choosing to expand globally.

There are two sectors that might be called first movers (or sector preemptors): luxury (LVMH and its fifty brands, Gucci, Armani, Prada, Calvin Klein, Ralph Lauren and many more), and high-volume hyper-markets (Carrefour, Wal-Mart and Tesco).

Now, with the more technologically advanced and easier global distribution capabilities of Wave III, as well as increasing wealth in many of the emerging countries, particularly China, the luxury and volume-priced brands and retailers are simply accelerating their expansion.

Among the luxury sector, some, like Prada (the luxury men's and women's apparel and accessory brand based in Italy), are expanding in very creative ways, elevating the "neuroexperience" to a preemptive level. They created what they call Prada Epicenters, specially designed stores for which the store itself is a piece of art. And each store is unique. The first Epicenter was launched in Tokyo in 2003 and has subsequently been rolled out in New York and Beverly Hills. Consumers visit these stores just to experience the art museum-like environment.

Another neurological connecting initiative by Prada was the launching of online auctions for exclusive products in 2006; they then followed that up with a series of film projects, including a beautifully artistic film titled *Trembled Blossoms*. Even though these films are important enough in their own right, the fact that they are being produced by a luxury fashion brand—and shown in their stores and on their websites—lends credence to the power of the new digital world; indeed, it is a threat to traditional film distribution. And in Seoul, Korea, in 2009 Prada launched the Transformer, a specially designed art house of new designs and films, which for six months had over 100,000 visitors. During its last few weeks the whole exhibit was turned over to art students to utilize the facility for their own creations.

Another example of a luxury brand using innovative strategies to expand its global footprint while also elevating its experience to a neurologically connecting level is Lebau Hotel and Resorts. As a part of its global preemptive distribution strategy, Lebau teaches a course in a number of business schools worldwide on how it creates its own unique, highly elevated luxury experience. After all, with room rates as high as $10,000 per night, Lebau figures it had better capture a share of the minds of those young, soon-to-be business leaders from which much of their future business will likely be generated. Similar to Prada, they also use art as a traffic builder. For this reason alone, a visit to The Dome in Bangkok is considered a "must" for global luxury travelers.

On the other end of the retail spectrum is the global preemptive distribution race in the volume-priced supermarket space, as competitors seek to establish primary positions in each region. In China, for example, Wal-Mart, Tesco and Carrefour are all competing against local Chinese supermarkets to gain dominant share. Furthermore, they are building infrastructure to support further expansion.

This is occurring across Asia. Vietnam continues to liberalize expansion opportunities that both Wal-Mart and Carrefour are taking advantage of. Obviously, by taking major share early on in these countries' growth trajectories, it will be increasingly difficult for new competitors to threaten the dominant positions of these giants when the markets begin to mature.

Target Stores, long exclusive to the United States, is also considering global expansion in Canada, Mexico and Latin America.

Does the global expansion of these supermarkets send a message to the department-store sector? If they don't begin to figure out how to preemptively leverage their brands globally, will the window of opportunity close?

The newest catalyst and opportunity for global expansion are the emerging and rapidly growing middle classes in the developing countries. These markets are ripe for many of the more mainstream brands and retailers such as Gap, American Eagle Outfitters Inc., The North Face, Abercrombie & Fitch, Iconix's Candie's stores and Bebe Stores. Even Macy's is considering China as a potential global expansion opportunity, according to an article in the *Chicago Tribune*.[2] Others, such as Lee and Wrangler jeans, Levi Strauss & Co., Guess Jeans and Nike footwear, are already established in many of those markets and will continue to expand.

Among all the emerging markets, China is a primary target, with its middle class projected to reach 700 million people by 2020 according to Euromonitor, an international retail market research firm.

The head of Gap's Asia-Pacific region, John Ermantinger, spoke of his firm's China strategy in a 2010 *Women's Wear Daily* article. Of Gap's $14 billion plus in sales, roughly 10 percent comes from its international business. However, they expect China to become the cornerstone of its global strategy. Ermantinger clearly sees Gap preempting its competitors. He stated, "There are a lot of brands in China, but in our space, there is not an American representation yet so Gap is looking forward to being that authentic purveyor of casual apparel."[3]

In the same *Women's Wear Daily* article, it was cited that Nike, over the past thirty years, has gained the largest share of athletic footwear in China, having reached almost $500 million in sales in 2010. Guess Jeans anticipates a five-fold increase in stores, from 40 to 200 between 2010 and 2015. Iconix envisions the number of Candie's stores growing from 50 to 500 over the same period. And VF Corporation projects a 40 percent increase in the distribution of its Lee and Wrangler brands through its roughly 400 stores over the next five years.

Another less recognized advantage to operating globally is the ability to discover new successful strategies that can then be fed back into their home markets. For example, Best Buy purchased the chain Car Warehouse in the United Kingdom so that they could bring their concept and the skills back to the United States as well as into other countries where they may compete.

Those brands that have global consumer recognition, and that control their value chains—such as Starbucks, McDonald's, Ralph Lauren, Calvin Klein, The North Face as well as many others— have already made global inroads and are accelerating their expansions. Even traditional retailers who have strong brand recognition, like Macy's, Neiman-Marcus and others, are beginning to craft international strategies.

On a final note, regardless of the degree to which any consumer-facing business is planning or actually implementing global expansion, the sense of urgency to do so has never been higher. In those countries experiencing the highest sustainable rates of growth, they provide an open field for those seeking early preemption of dominant share. How long the opportunity lasts before market congestion sets in is an unknown. So every consumer business should have a matrix of global markets prioritized by market attractiveness (that is, size, growth, competitive intensity, etc.) for their products and services, the potential mix of distribution options for that market (including all of the latest digital platforms) and the investment required to support different options. Those that succeed in executing these global priorities will be those that thrive.

CHAPTER 7

THE IMPORTANCE OF VALUE CHAIN CONTROL

THE BOTTOM-LINE WINNERS

Given our thesis that neither preemptive distribution nor neuro-connection with consumers would be possible without a business having total control of its value chain, we feel it's necessary to discuss the concept in more depth, and develop a way of measuring its relative importance for achieving success, especially since we also know that the first two principles are nearly impossible to measure quantitatively, because of their subjectivity and numerous variables. Control of the value chain, on the other hand, is both objective and measurable—and proves to be the game changer for many companies.

It is important to make a distinction between how we define supply chain vs. value chain. Supply chain is typically defined as the back end of the business: the set of issues around the flow of goods or materials, the transportation network, logistics, distribution centers and the handling of the goods inside the distribution centers. However, we define the value chain more broadly, encompassing issues such as who creates the value, where it's created and where and how it's marketed, including its ultimate point-of-sale (all activities of the front end of the business).

The value chain is what we call a never-ending, fully integrated, virtuous cycle, starting with the consumer, pausing at point of consumption and then starting all over again (see Figure 7.1). There are three continuous and simultaneous steps in the process:

- **Define:** Identifying and defining what consumers expect from, or even desire beyond expectations of, the brand. This is ongoing, using all research methodologies, including sales tracking, in-store interaction and testing. In essence, the real winners virtually live with their consumers 24/7. This process continually affirms the brand's core value, suggests improvements and guides new value creation and innovation. A clear point of competitive differentiation for the brand is articulated. If well executed, this process will yield a deep metaphor for what the true essence of the brand stands for and what the consumer is seeking.
- **Develop:** Developing the value starts with using knowledge gained from research to conceptually plan for new and/or improved value (brands), then on to actual value development, including the neurological experience. Also, in this cycle, the highly integrated, seamless and demand-driven "back end" segment of the chain (as described later in the chapter) will provide continually innovative productivity strategies, while the integrated marketing or "front end" of the chain will continually innovate or strengthen the marketing strategies.
- **Delivery:** The final cycle in the virtuous loop is the preemptive, precise and perpetual distribution of the value, along with its neurological experience. It's also critical that the value (brand) creator has maximum control of this final cycle in the loop, control of its presentation and experience

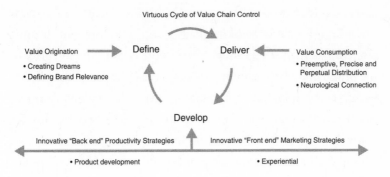

Figure 7.1: Virtuous cycle of value chain control

at point-of-sale, which also includes line size, mix, frequency, flow of goods and as much of the operations as possible (sales and service).

As we mentioned earlier, total control of the value chain does not necessarily mean owning every function in the chain. In fact, in our commercially globalized world, one would be hard-pressed to find many vertically integrated *and* vertically owned value chains. In apparel, Spain-based Inditex comes close by owning most of its production, and a few large Chinese apparel manufacturers own their retail distribution in China (for more on their future intentions to acquire brands and distribution in the United States, see chapter 8). But for the most part, globalization has driven the production operations of most industries to lower-cost manufacturing in emerging countries.

However, while some functions in the value chain such as production or distribution *will most likely* be shared, the entity that originates, owns and/or creates the brand (whether retailer, wholesaler or service provider) must have dominant control, or at least be relentlessly pursuing it. Most important, it must control those parts of the chain that directly connect with, or "touch," the consumer. After all, continuous innovation emanates from tracking and responding to consumers' ever-changing desires; so the dominant brand must control origination and development. It must also control marketing, which ensures the continuing integrity of the brand and its consumers' expectations. It must control distribution to gain preemptive access to consumers geographically and strategically on all relevant distribution platforms. And finally, control of the point-of-sale is perhaps most essential of all, as it allows the brand to create the emotionally connecting experience we have found to be so critical. Apple, Ralph Lauren, Starbucks and Disney are examples of brands that may share control in various functions of their value chains, but that exercise dominant control over all those functions that connect with the consumer: creation, innovation, marketing, distribution and point-of-sale.

The following is our analysis of the key elements of value-chain control and its correlation between degree of control and relative success between various retail models.

Core Elements of Value-Chain Control

As we studied the various retail as well as branded wholesale and service models, similarities emerged in how they defined "control" and how their process was driven by three core elements. Our first discovery was that while some discussed controlling parts of their chains, others never used the word "control." And none, in fact, articulated a proactive strategy of totally controlling their value chains to achieve preemptive distribution and provide the optimum experience at the point-of-sale. Every one of those poised to be winning brands and retailers, however, were aggressively pursuing and implementing those strategies.

Ralph Lauren's declarations of controlling destiny, have been, and still are, manifested by their buying back their many licensees (for control), continually increasing their retail business (now accounting for about 50 percent of total revenues) and insisting that retail customers cede control of the presentation and operations in their designated store space. As mentioned in the Introduction regarding retail expansion and brand control, Eric Wiseman, CEO of VF Corporation (which includes The North Face, Vans, Nautica and others), stated in the annual report "We want to continue to present the brand in ways we can control."[1] The VF Corporation also continues to increase its retail business. Home Shopping Network CEO Mindy Grossman sprinkles the use of "control" throughout her numerous public presentations of "knowing what our consumers want, where, when and how they want it, so we've got to create and control the distribution and experience for her."[2] And JCPenney CEO Myron "Mike" Ullman may not specifically articulate controlling JCPenney's value chain, but it is most certainly moving in that direction while it aggressively pursues growing its stable of highly successful (and "controlled") private brands (estimated to be over 40 percent of total revenues), as are Macy's, Kohl's and others.

As we pursued the CEOs' varied expressions of the importance of control, we were able to discern several common objectives they were attempting to achieve through implementing greater control of their value chains. Again, and not surprising to us, we discovered their end-game to be in synch with our thesis, but with their own choice of words.

Control provides greater flexibility and enables rapid responses and adaptation to shifts in the marketplace, such as changes in consumer desires, the structure of the marketplace and competitive strategies and positioning. Tactically, control enables quick response to changes in required volume levels, inventory build-up and flow, to name a few.

As articulated in our thesis, the key objective of value chain control is to create and control the preemptive distribution of a neurologically connective experience all the way through to its consumption, including the all-important point-of-sale.

Another commonly expressed objective was to control the key components of the value chain that create the most value, and therefore are more vulnerable to competitors. In other words, they need control to leverage those parts that drive share gain, revenues and profitability. This corresponds to our thesis of controlling those elements in the value chain that directly connect with and/or serve the consumer. These are the beginning of the chain to gain knowledge about the consumer (their behavior, wants and desires, and what they are dreaming of); the creation of that dream and its experience; and the final point-of-sale for optimum presentation of the dream and the experience.

Finally, the company needs the alignment of the entire organization, as well as external suppliers, to accomplish these objectives. This may seem obvious, but it was interesting that most of the leaders we spoke with referred to the challenge of balancing competing requirements. In many cases the tradeoffs did not necessarily optimize value chain effectiveness. For example, Zappos would not manage costs at the expense of the customer experience.

Likewise, Amazon realized that to meet its defined customer experience of rapid and reliable shipping, it would need to build excess capacity. The reason for this is driven by simple math (actually complex math) that as demand becomes more variable along with growing product variety, and as capacity utilization increases, lead times increase in a nonlinear fashion. In other words, without building excess capacity, Amazon would fail on its promise of timely delivery. If Amazon did not have this insight—along with the two objectives cited above and the understanding of the need for value chain control to accomplish all of it—then the investment in extra capacity would not have been justified.

Having identified these objectives, our next challenge was to identify a coherent set of principles that would provide companies with the ability to successfully achieve them.

In managing the globalized supply chain, there are a whole series of key elements that are critical and fundamental to the effectiveness of the organization. These elements include managing the complexity of lead times and volatile costs, be they transportation or commodity prices, to name two. Depending on where goods are sourced, the size of the order and its shipment can have an enormous impact on costs and the complexity of managing the chain. For example, as energy prices have risen so have transportation costs (by about 50 percent between 2002 and 2008). During that same period, there was a commensurate increase of about 60 percent in inventory per vessel being shipped.[3] Therefore, the cost of transportation slowed the average response time as, increasingly, only fully loaded vessels were utilized.

Effective supply-chain management has many other elements that are obviously critical: risk management strategies; sustainability, or how to be "greener"; how to support different business models (that is, online supply chain requirements are quite different than those for regular retail stores); or simply how to manage costs. However, none of these suggests a comprehensive method or definition of how to measure value chain control across the entire spectrum of different business models.

So our research led us to three common characteristics that we believe define value chain control for all segments, whether the primary source of value are low cost products or high fashion.

Regardless of the degree of control—from Zara on one end, with almost total vertical integration, to the Wrangler wholesale denim brand selling primarily through Wal-Mart on the other extreme—we determined that the successful companies all focused on the following three core elements, which, when implemented, did give them greater control over their value chains. This required a total strategy, because these three elements if implemented separately might result in tactical or short term advantages, but would never result in total control. The execution must occur simultaneously. The elements are:

1. Increasing Collaboration (Leveraging Human, Intellectual and Physical Assets across the Entire Value Chain)

Consumers

The winners are obsessed with understanding what their ultimate consumers are dreaming of, continuously tracking and researching consumer responses to identify where new and different tactics are needed. Much of the best collaboration with consumers comes from the interaction at the point-of-sale, where the experience is happening and consumers can actually co-create new ideas along with the brand. For example, in lululemon stores there is a chalkboard by the changing rooms for consumers to jot down any feedback they might have after trying the clothes on. Then on a regular basis the store managers have a conference call with their design and production teams to share and discuss any action they should take on these consumer insights. Apple is also a great example because the store design, the employees' roles and the products themselves are all created to enable consumers to develop their own experience in its stores and of course beyond the stores. It is not uncommon to see people spending time at the Genius Bar to discuss service issues, others getting a tutorial on how to use the products to complete a project via the One to One service, children playing games on a special kids computer and finally everybody else testing and experimenting with the latest products all on display and easy to use. Each visit offers a unique and engaging learning experience. Each purchase, be it an iPod, iPhone, iPad or otherwise, is then customized by each consumer to reflect their individual tastes and desires through the app store or iTunes. This is one of the best examples of a co-creation of experiences with Apple as the platform.

Another example is the highly popular television show *American Idol*. Its format makes the audience a central part of the show—everybody is eligible to vote for their favorite. The audience determines the outcome, and communities rally around their hometown contestants as the weeks progress, building excitement and a compelling narrative. The show owes its success to collaboration as much as anything.

Vendors and Customers

When it came to externalizing the creation, marketing, distribution and ultimate selling of the brand, the most successful companies had intense, and in some cases exclusive, collaborations. Whole Foods employs a full-time food forager to continually identify and bring to market new products that are being developed by small producers, which are often more responsive to new consumer trends in the grocery sector. Whole Foods will even provide financing to producers who need capital to grow.[4] This exploration is also a continual source for private and/or exclusive products. H&M, Forever 21 and Uniqlo, for example, where "fast fashion" (reduced, rapid-line cycles) is their primary competitive advantage and a major part of their "experience," make it a priority to ensure that their manufacturers understand that, and direct all their efforts toward supporting this advantage. VF Corporation, with its diverse portfolio of brands, has a strategy called the "Third Way," a hybrid of complete supply-chain control and relationships with suppliers (this process is explained in greater detail when we take a closer look at VF Corporation in chapter 10). All the marketing, advertising, packaging and communications vendors are collaborative partners, which communicate daily with their counterparts within the branded companies. This ensures that everyone is on the same page in creating, developing and maintaining the brand's DNA and its presentation to the consumer. Similarly, the close collaborative relationships between the department stores and their "exclusive" and private brand vendors are essential for controlling the timely flow of goods, presentation, environment and experience.

Internal Partners

Wave I and Wave II value chains were organized around traditional functional silos. Production would manage and operate its business according to stated goals, with no understanding of, or dialogue with, the other silos—marketing, distribution, sales and so forth—all of which also operated according to their own goals. There was no integration or collaborative control, and the entire chain was driven by a forecasting model that "pushed" goods first into warehouses, then into stores, with the hope that their forecasts were right. In Wave III, those businesses still operating with this model are hurtling toward extinction. An old phrase coined by one of those still-breathing dinosaurs is "Pile it high and hope it will fly."

The Wave III winners transformed their organizations into matrices of collaborative integration across all functions of the organization. Strategic planning, research, design, product development, operations, forecasting, production, logistics, distribution, marketing and often finance, HR and other staff functions operated with a holistic view: a clear understanding of the brand's consumer, and their function's contribution to driving the ultimate brand promise. These chains are tightly controlled because all participants are operating under the same brand-to-consumer-driven objectives and strategies.

A final note on internal collaboration is that nowhere across the value chain is it more critical than in the integration and management of the multidistribution platforms now necessary to gain preemptive distribution. The winners will turn this complex matrix into a powerful synergy, allowing the consumer to be able to cross over easily from one to the other for different purposes: research, buying, returning and customer service, whether they are stationary or on the move.

2. Shrinking Decision Times (Accelerating and Optimizing Good Decisions on How to Execute against Target Value Proposition)

The second element that we felt defined having control over the value chain was the ability to shrink decision times across the chain. This is another hallmark of a highly collaborative organization. Shrinking decision times made possible the "speed-to-market" models, which require shorter product development cycles and the agility to rapidly respond to marketplace shifts. And while Mango and the fast-fashion examples again come to mind, the concept is broader than merely getting new and fresh product to the market more often. It describes a culture that is consistently improving its responsiveness and organizational feedback loops to make better decisions. From an evolutionary perspective, organisms that are able to detect and respond to stimuli quicker have won out in natural selection. This quicker response is directly correlated to the degree of control a business has over its value chain.

While this element is organic in the fast-fashion business models, their counterparts in the specialty branded retail sector (Aeropostale, Chico's, Victoria's Secret and others) also have highly controlled value chains, thanks to their direct connection with consumers. Their feedback loops are also quick, providing more responsive and quicker decision cycles. And the department stores are finding that the greater control they exercise over their private and exclusive brands, the more they can reduce cycle times, increase flexibility and responsiveness to consumer changes, turn out more new lines more often and more easily localize their lines by store. This also increases differentiation and allows for greater pricing flexibility. Most important, its impact on productivity, the lifeblood of all retailing, is enormous.

3. Creating the Demand-Responsive, Efficient Value Chain (By Minimizing Inventory and Ensuring the Continual Flow of Goods)

This final element would not be possible without the synergy created by the first two: collaborative integration and rapid decision making. The best companies we analyzed had core processes that could be defined as seamless, simultaneous, fast, flexible, responsive and cost-efficient. The key elements that we identified included multiple supply chains for different products, a built-in redundancy to manage significant demand variability and sustained investments in anything that increased speed and responsiveness. The successful business was driven by consumer demand—what consumers are actually buying, as opposed to what companies choose to push to comply with forecasting. The entire business is organized, managed and operated around a brand-to-consumer objective.

In this controlled, demand-responsive process, the product literally never sleeps. And in a wonderful ancillary benefit, this eliminates the old nemesis of too much inventory, which the old forecasting model inevitably resulted in. Instead, it provides more and smaller lots (responsive to consumers' demands for newness more often), speeds the flow of goods so they are not sitting idle (both in the warehouse and on the balance sheet) and enables rapid replenishment. It also decreases markdowns, increases productivity and, most important, keeps the consumer happily coming back to see what's new.

There are great examples of organizations developing these processes. In fact, in the last ten years, according to *Kurt Salmon Associates'* Product Sourcing Benchmarking Database, 2010, leaders in the apparel industry shrank product development times by more than 40 percent. In the digital world, process breakthroughs are even more visible. Amazon altered an entire industry by redefining the process of book distribution through its Kindle. This also fundamentally changed consumers' expectations about both speed of access and price. The Kindle was simply a new spin-off of Amazon's entire enterprise, which was *the* original, game-changing retail model of online ordering and low-cost shipping optimization.

Amazon also increased its response times and efficiency by building its distribution centers close to UPS shipping locations. This actually utilized all three principles described in this chapter, and gained huge competitive advantage over all other e-commerce sites.

Measuring the Bottom-Line Winners

Having defined the key elements of value chain control, we wanted to go one step further. In order to substantiate our thesis, we decided to develop metrics to measure the correlation between control of the value chain and success.

We randomly picked retailers from the following segments: apparel, auto parts, consumer electronics, department stores, home improvements and furnishings, food retailers, drugstores and sporting goods stores.

In 2007 we asked industry consultants and executives to rank the companies that they were most familiar with on each of the three criteria that we have just defined.[5] We then combined the ratings from all our sources (believing in the wisdom of crowds) and created an overall rating for each retailer.

Finally, we correlated these ratings against changes in market capitalization (company value) of the companies analyzed. We also assigned each retailer to one of four groups (ranked from good to poor) depending upon their overall rating.

The entire project was fraught with methodological challenges. The first pitfall we wanted to avoid was selection bias. There is a natural tendency for people to automatically give high marks to successful companies on any measured attribute because they will assume that the current success must surely be driven by the attribute that is being measured. After all, who can forget that up until its collapse, Enron was regularly rewarded for being one of the best run and most admired companies. This accolade was awarded, it now appears, because they were very profitable. So the logic was circular: because they were profitable everyone believed that Enron must be well run. They were not. To avoid this bias, we decided not to include in our sample those companies that had high profiles and were generally perceived as being extraordinarily successful. So, for example, Apple and Wal-Mart were not included.

Our second challenge was to avoid having one or two companies weighing disproportionately on our results. In fact, we sought comparable groups of companies in terms of market value that had significantly different ratings in terms of their level of control. So in each group, the starting point of measured market value for the top three quartiles were all relatively close, with no one dominant company. In other words, there was no one company within a quartile whose trajectory would determine the overall outcomes.

Finally, in order to further cleanse the data, we asked our experts to rank the three individual principles; however, to do so only if they were familiar with that specific area. By combining all of the results together we felt the probability of bias would be substantially diminished.

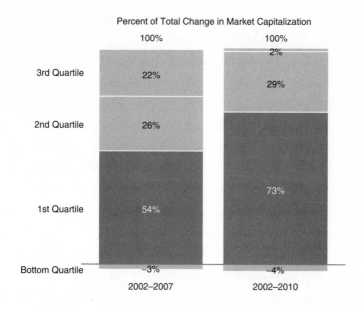

Figure 7.2: The 1st quartile of stores accounts for 73 percent change in market cap from 2002 to 2010

Our research found that companies exercising maximum and/or total control over their entire value chains created significantly higher economic returns than those that did not. In our analysis the correlation between changes in market capitalization and the retailer's score was both statistically significant and explained close to 40 percent of the change in market value.

Between 2002 and 2010, in our sample companies, the first quartile was responsible for 73 percent of the total economic value created by the sample. This was particularly impressive since they represented only just over one-third of the actual market value of the sample at the beginning of 2002.

Additionally, during the recession, ca. 2007, 25 percent of the bottom quartile went bankrupt. In no other group did any company fail. The data suggest that to thrive or even survive requires achieving control of the value chain. Accordingly, we predict that over 50 percent of retailers in our sample will eventually fail because they are not moving fast enough toward this goal. The bottom half of our sample is full of likely candidates.

Interestingly, in our first quartile there are a mix of companies that we believe also excel in preemptive distribution and making neurological connections with their consumers. However, we believe that there are others that are in the early stages of evolving to a stronger execution on those dimensions. For some (most notably Aeropostale), a focus on operational excellence enabled them to accelerate past their competitors during this period, opening the door to a substantially enhanced consumer connection.

Moreover, because this study was conducted in 2007, by 2010 we could see how the companies performed through the Great Recession. Not surprisingly, those retailers in the bottom half of the sample found that they were still unable to create any economic value, while those in the top group remained the largest creators of economic value (albeit somewhat diminished). Obviously, all companies lost value during the downturn. However, even as consumers' priorities shifted during the recession (for example, away from aspirational luxury), we still found that retailers with high scores on value-chain control outperformed others, regardless of sector.

Also not surprising, though sad, was the discovery that the companies that had disappeared by 2010 (for example, Circuit City, CSK Auto, etc.) had been rated in the bottom quartile in 2007. In no other quartile had this happened. While the reasons for each company's demise are manifold and various, it's a strong possibility that if they had implemented a stronger, more controlled value chain, they might have survived.

In summary, while control of the value chain does not necessarily guarantee perpetual success, (e.g., Gap, Starbucks and others), inability to achieve it will guarantee failure.

CHAPTER 8

WHAT IT ALL MEANS

CONTROL, COLLABORATION, COLLAPSE AND THE CHINESE

The sweeping changes we've described in the retail sector are just the beginning. Their implications will reverberate across all consumer-facing industries well into the future, and the new models will evolve alongside technology and consumer preference.

In fact, as the companies we researched and their counterparts continue to change their business models around our three operating principles, the aggregate transformation will reinvent entire industry structures. In this chapter, we discuss what we believe some of those changes will be.

The Collapse of the Traditional Retail/Wholesale Business Model

You already know our Wave III mantra—the consumer is central and literally holds all the cards of commerce. We described how this evolved from a time when retailers and brands *were* central, and not widely distributed, so that consumers had to seek them out. Back then, it was also more efficient and effective for products and services to join together in one location (the store), and to provide the consumer with the widest possible selection of merchandise. This aggregation model also expanded into mall and shopping center structures. During this period, since the retail store was the compelling draw for consumers and knew better than the wholesalers what its consumers wanted, it was more efficient and effective for the retailer to edit, purchase and present the wholesalers' goods.

That scenario no longer exists, and the jointly shared retail/wholesale relationship is both inefficient and ineffective for several reasons.

For one thing, it makes control of the value chain much more challenging, for both retailers and wholesalers. In turn, this severely challenges the ability of either one to execute preemptive distribution or achieve neurological connectivity. It's not impossible, but it's much more difficult.

For those who create the products and brands, the primary challenge is being able to control, influence or create the selling environment. The selling environment, of course, is where the brand must neurologically connect with the consumer, deploying the entire imagery and DNA of the brand. The traditional model affords those brand creators only limited access to consumers and the subtle shifts in their behaviors, desires and aspirations. Thus the brand will not be totally responsive in making the continual refinements and improvements necessary to stay connected to the consumer. If all the store interactions around the consumer are lost to the channel partner, this most valuable consumer feedback does not become part of the brand development cycle.

The complexities of implementing a new consumer experience through preexisting distribution networks, which must also address multiple demands from many other brands and products across multiple categories, are immense. The decisions wholesalers must make about how much to invest in their "channel partners" (retailers), as opposed to their end customers, is also vexing. Which channel partners should they focus on? How do they develop a relationship that allows them more control over their brand and how it's mixed, presented and serviced throughout the store? How can they communicate with and be responsive to their end consumers, now that they are highly mobile and difficult to reach? All this makes for a slower, more cumbersome, less agile organization, resulting in a huge disconnect between brand and consumer.

For the traditional retailer, the same challenges exist, as they turn their focus to establishing their own neurological connection between customers and their store brand (e.g., Macy's), as well as preemptively gaining access to consumers ahead of their competitors. Saddled with their traditional brick-and-mortar model, in a world where consumers no longer have to leave the house, how do they transform themselves to better connect with consumers to gain the market share they need to survive? What is it that their store brand stands for and how does their current product selection and in-store experience reflect this? How quickly can they respond to new, more agile competitors like Internet retailers and specialty chain brands, some of which carry the same wholesale brands they do?

From a tactical perspective, it's complicated. How long is the planning process and how big the investment to develop a new format, highlight a particular "experience" or experiment with new product/consumer segments as well as new distribution platforms?

The decline of the traditional retail/wholesale model can also be tracked by its financial performance over the past twenty years. By the measure of continuous share loss alone, this performance strongly suggests the trend will continue toward ultimate collapse.

Traditional department stores lost 50 percent of their market share between 1990 and 2010. There were also several notable bankruptcies during that period, among them Alexander's, B. Altman, The Broadway, Ohrbach's, Halle Brothers, McCrory's, Woodward

& Lothrop, Mervyns, Gottschalks and many more. Between 1997 and 2010, sales through the traditional sector fell by around 5 percent per year, transferring those $12 billion of sales to the specialty retail stores.

In the apparel sector it was even worse. As we discussed, since its inception in the 1960s, the apparel specialty chain model grew faster and gained more share each year than all other retail sectors. Having surpassed department stores, which in 1987 held the number one share at over 30 percent, the apparel retail specialists owned close to 35 percent by the early 2000s. Department stores' share of apparel has dropped below 18 percent and continues to fall, along with the number of major department stores, which is down from about 59 in 1989 to under 10 in 2010.[1]

Perhaps the most compelling example is what happened in the teen apparel market. From the late 1990s until the beginning of the recession, there was an explosion of teen apparel retailers, and the rate of growth for dollars spent on teen apparel grew at an incredible 14 percent per year. The growth of specialty retailers like American Eagle, Aeropostale, Zumiez and the pricey Abercrombie & Fitch all gained substantial share from the department stores over this period. The growth came from their ability to effectively create highly engaging, unique environments for their target consumers, which department stores could not match, because of their lumbering business model. The ability of the specialty retailers to execute these strategies, of course, sprang from their tightly controlled value chains.

Other examples of the importance of value-chain control and the execution of our three principles abound. One of the major reasons for Circuit City's demise was its decision to cut costs by eliminating its version of Best Buy's "blue shirts," a highly trained team of store associates devoted to top-notch service and consumer education. Thus Circuit City completely lost the neurological connector that Best Buy went on to uniquely own, and even expand upon with its "Geek Squad." It also lost on preemptive distribution by failing to localize, which Best Buy has achieved so remarkably well through its small "neighborhood" store formats. Finally, Circuit City failed to pursue a private or exclusive branding program, as Best Buy is doing with its Insignia home theater systems and blu-ray players, Dynex webcams and Init equipment bags, among others. Without value-chain control, it also lost pricing flexibility, and was forced to give up chunks of business to Wal-Mart, Best Buy and the Internet players.

Inside the traditional department stores, one of the key strategic thrusts over the period of 2005–2010 has been to take more control of the value chain by attaining exclusive distribution of wholesale brands and creating privately owned brands. Those who are winning have the ability to execute this strategy successfully. Kohl's private and exclusive brands are estimated to account for over 40 percent of sales, JCPenney's over 50 percent, Macy's over 40 percent, and although Wal-Mart does not like to report it, its private and exclusive brands are estimated at over 50 percent. The largest stores have already partly destroyed the distinction between retailer and wholesaler.

As stated in chapter 4, National Panel Data identified that in 1975, 25 percent of all apparel sold were private or exclusive brands, reaching 50 percent in 2005. It projected this amount to reach 60 percent by 2010.

This realization is also driving the investments of many of the traditional wholesale brands. Ralph Lauren has stated a commitment to expand its direct-to-consumer retail business, now close to 50 percent of revenues. VF Corporation, one of the largest makers of denim (Wrangler, Lee, 7 For All Mankind), and owner of The North Face, Vans, Reef, Nautica and others, totally understands the imperative of controlling its preemptive connection to and with its consumers, compared to goods being cherry-picked and stacked on a shelf in a traditional store. As mentioned, it also aggressively pursues expansion of the retail component of its business. With the Wrangler brand, which is the second-largest seller of denim in Wal-Mart (after Wal-Mart's Faded Glory private brand), VF Corporation has embarked on a strategic test, launching a freestanding Wrangler store.

As both traditional retailers and wholesalers, then, accelerate their efforts to build their own brands and their own distinct connections with their consumers, while selling within the same space, conflicts are bound to increase. The traditional "partnership" at the point-of-sale to sell to the same consumer becomes a more divided effort, with each partner pursuing its own brand objectives. And, in doing so, they not only dilute their respective messages, they severely weaken the most vital part of the chain: the part that connects with the ultimate consumer.

How will this tug of war play out?

An early visionary who successfully wrestled with these issues was Paul Charron. He was appointed CEO of Liz Claiborne in 1995 and chairman a year later. After stabilizing the declining business, he proceeded to profitably grow it to be the fourth-largest in its sector. The reality of managing this unprecedented growth was wed to Charron's view of how the dynamics of retail/wholesale relationships would ultimately evolve. And as Liz Claiborne Inc. grew into a portfolio of both retail and wholesale brands, the complexity of running both business models provided him with a clearer view of what we are now describing as a "collapsing relationship."

One of the key challenges that these experiences highlighted was how to maintain the organizational flexibility, creativity and management of a portfolio of brands; specifically, how to be excellent as both a wholesaler and retailer. In a world with an infinite number of finite market segments, Charron was arguably the first to realize the power of a portfolio strategy to be able to preemptively target and distribute to an infinite number of opportunistic segments. Further, Liz Claiborne under Charron was a pioneer in leveraging their huge back-end operating platform to scale and gain productivity synergies to service the highly complex and segmented front end (brand marketing) of the business. It also provided the leveraging of intelligence from one segment against opportunities in related but different segments. Regarding this breakthrough model, Charron said, "It's a great concept. But, if you can't control it, it can become a nightmare."[2] The assignment for those who follow Charron's strategic insight is to make the operational model excel. In chapter 10 on VF we explore how this leader is architecting the model.

Collapse through Conversion

Even as we predict the collapse of the traditional model, we believe the enlightened and strategically savvy retailers and wholesalers that understand this conundrum will manage its collapse together and convert the "old" model into a new. Those that do not will disappear.

We believe the former group will take several paths, including the following:

1. The wholesale brands will pursue, and the retailers will relinquish, control of the brand's product, service, presentation and ultimately sales within the store. There will likely be a new kind of financial arrangement, perhaps leasing with some top- or bottom-line sharing.

    For instance, Macy's, a go-to brand in its own right, will cede space ownership and control to traditional wholesale brands (Ralph Lauren, for example) and even other retail brands, such as Sunglass Hut. JCPenney is doing something similar with Mango and Sephora. In other retail and wholesale sectors, the control at point-of-sale will not be so easily separated.

    For example, as cited earlier, the Wrangler brand may never operate a Wrangler "store" per se, in space it would lease within Wal-Mart. But because the Wrangler brand is more knowledgeable than Wal-Mart about its core consumers (what they want, where, when and how often, including different product preferences of consumers shopping different Wal-Mart stores), and because Wrangler's superior supply-chain process is so rapid and responsive, Wal-Mart currently permits Wrangler to manage and control its line mix and size, frequency, replenishment and presentation. We believe that this trend will expand.

In fact, Wrangler's management of its space provides additional nonfinancial value to the partnership by creating a synergy that strengthens Wrangler's long-term position with Wal-Mart.

Of course, this strong partnership does not preclude or impede Wrangler's testing its own freestanding branded stores, which may ultimately be rolled out into its core consumers' neighborhoods, exercising the principle of pre-emptive distribution even to the exclusion of its strategic retail partner.

Another example is Proctor & Gamble. Like Wrangler, P&G's vaunted research and marketing prowess gives it unparalleled knowledge about its consumers; its supply-chain logistics and distribution skills are also superior. All this (along with slotting fees where appropriate) qualifies its brands for control over mix, size, frequency, replenishment and presentation within its retail partners' stores.

While P&G may not have a freestanding store strategy in its immediate future, we do not rule out the possibility. It recently opened a "pop-up" store in New York, (leased a space for a limited period of time), at the location (according to its data) of the highest coupon-redemption area of the city. The stores provide a brand experience: Customers can have their hair washed and conditioned with Pantene, get a makeover from Olay and Cover Girl and shop through a kitchen and laundry area where Tide, Bounce, Dawn and Downy are on display.

We even asked ourselves, now that P&G owns the Gillette brands, why it couldn't either open barbershops or be allocated space within other retailers' stores for an experiential shaving or grooming area? After all, as reported in the *Cincinnati Times,* it is already launching similar concepts:

> Agile Pursuits Franchising, a P&G subsidiary, is looking to open Tide Dry Cleaners for the two cities, which would employ 15 to 20 people per location. Tide Dry Cleaners began in 2008, with a pilot of three dry cleaner stores in Kansas City.
>
> P&G's Agile Pursuits Franchising entered the car wash business in 2007 with P&G's Mr. Clean brand, and now is the largest full-service U.S. car wash franchise, with 16 locations in Ohio, Georgia and Texas; another seven facilities are under development.
>
> "Entering the franchise and service market is a model we find very attractive, as shown by the Mr. Clean Car Wash operations," said Jeff Wampler, general manager for Tide Dry Cleaners, in a press release issued by Procter & Gamble on Tuesday May 25, 2010. "Expanding our interests into the services industry helps us to reach more consumers' lives with outstanding service we know consumers are looking for and need."[3]

2. Wholesale brands will continue to launch and/or expand their direct-to-consumer retail businesses, on multidistribution platforms. These platforms include e-commerce, TV and cobranding with different branded product categories, but with similar consumer positioning for synergy (e.g., The North Face product in Lucy activewear stores). We believe these brands' retail business could eventually reach 80 percent of their total revenues.

It's important to keep in mind that a direct-to-consumer retail distribution strategy for traditional wholesale brands does not mean they will relinquish their retail "partnership" business. They will simply control those relationships, as mentioned above.

3. Traditional retail brands (e.g., Macy's, JCPenney and others) will continue their aggressive pursuit of private and/or exclusive brands. We believe their share of total revenues could reach 80 percent as well. In addition to differentiation, having control of these brands affords greater responsiveness, flexibility, reduced cycle time and an ability to turn out more new lines, more often. They can better "localize" according to consumer tastes, and they control the better part of two profit margins, providing greater pricing flexibility.

    Supermarkets offer a great example of how this is starting to play out. Consider O Organics. Owned by Safeway, O Organics (a private label brand) has gradually been replacing the niche and fringe brands offering organic produce. In fact, the private label produce of Safeway is crowding out the branded products, like Earthbound and Wallaby yogurts, across the board. In the future, the new private and/or exclusive brands will not be positioned as cheaper and almost as good as the branded products. They will be *as* good (or better) and priced accordingly.

4. As we mentioned previously, the traditional retailers will also seek higher productivity through leasing space (or other financial arrangements) to other retail brands whose consumer positioning is compatible, and whose presence would create a synergy. The logic and strategic benefits are described below.

5. The traditional retail brands will adopt and/or expand on a strategy of rolling out smaller neighborhood stores, preemptively gaining access to more consumers, and better enabling them to make the consumer connection by localizing their offerings (e.g., Best Buy, Wal-Mart, Bloomingdale's, JCPenney and others).

6. They will also leverage the power of their growing private and/or exclusive brands, by rolling out smaller specialty retail chains, again increasing control over their value chains to create great "experiences."

7. These retailers will continue to explore new distribution platforms of opportunity, such as "pop-up" stores (JCPenney, Target and others), in-home marketing and event marketing, using innovative concepts such as mobile marketing and other preemptive distribution strategies.

8. We would be remiss not to acknowledge the world's largest online "department store," Amazon, and how we believe it will ultimately evolve according to our thesis. First of all, we do believe its enormous success so far is attributable to its following our three strategic criteria: the Amazon "experience"; preemptive distribution; and certainly control of its value chain.

    However, as traditional retail competitors increasingly hone their online experience and distribution, and as the rapid growth of new e-commerce competitors continues, Amazon's clear playing field is going to get crowded. Therefore we believe that it, too, will expand on our three operating strategies.

    Currently, the Amazon experience (and what keeps customers coming back) is quick and easy access, convenience, low prices (and no shipping charges) and speedy delivery ("Amazon Prime"). To date, Amazon's preemptive distribution advantage has been confined to the online platform.

    As competition ratchets up and Amazon searches new avenues for growth, therefore, we expect it to take preemptive distribution to another level by opening brick-and-mortar retail "showrooms," as discussed in chapter 6.

Retailers Will Become Enclosed "Mini-Malls" for Increased Productivity

Retail-space productivity (sales per square foot) is arguably one of the most important metrics for retailers to quickly assess the strength and growth rate of their business. As organic growth in the industry has steadily declined, driving retailers to increase market share, one such strategy is to focus on increasing productivity in underperforming space.

Unfortunately, we know that in the current slow-to-no-growth market, traditional strategies have become merely the price of entry. Simply restocking underperforming space with similar product, therefore, however new or better it might be, is not likely to result in either increased traffic or improved productivity.

So the new strategy involves management's defining its real estate as a mall owner would. Management seeks to lease space to other retailers, brands and/or services that will increase both traffic and productivity.

For example, while the department stores will continue to strengthen and control their nameplate brand and their private or exclusive brands, they will lease space and the control of it (operations and presentation) to compatible outside designer and national brands across various consumer products industries (e.g., Sephora's and Mango's dedicated space in JCPenney, Peet's Coffee & Tea within Raley's grocery stores, Sunglass Hut and LVMH in Macy's). Think about RadioShack's renting space to Apple or Nintendo. Selfridge's department store in London has leased most of its space to brands for many years, to brands such as Vivienne Westwood, Y3 and John Rocha, trendy street brands such as Energie, Abercrombie and Dolce and Gabbana, as well as most recently, DCL (Dermatologic Cosmetic Laboratories) Skin and the Blink Brow Bar. This model doubles as part of a brand's preemptive distribution strategy, accessing additional and new distribution platforms.

The benefits are great for both the retailer and the joined compatible business. The newly joined business gets immediate, low-capital invested growth in multiple locations, thereby reaching new customers geographically. It also benefits from the traffic generated by the host retailer. Likewise, the host retailer benefits from the destination traffic of the joined business. Finally, the combined businesses enhance the shopping experience and therefore mutually strengthen their consumer connections.

Taken to its logical end point over time, the collapse and/or conversion of the traditional departmentalized retailing model greatly consolidates the playing field. Thousands of currently weak, marginalized or commoditized wholesale brands will be eliminated, and the opportunity for creating new wholesale brands will be greatly diminished.

This transformed retail model will have space only for those wholesale power brands with global recognition (Coca-Cola, P&G, Ralph Lauren, LVMH and other designer-status brands), or brands whose level of innovation remains high in growth categories such as technology (Apple), action sports (Under Armour) or consumer package goods (P&G brands).

To emphasize this point, as Trader Joe's has demonstrated, even power brands as nationally entrenched as Peter Pan peanut butter are vulnerable to retailers owning the experience and creating their own brands.

At the end of the day, the collapse and convergence of the traditional retail/wholesale business model also eliminates even the function of the words "retail" and "wholesale." Because in the eyes of the consumer, those retailers and wholesalers that successfully transform their businesses will simply all be brands. Therefore they would more appropriately be defined as brand managers.

Fifty Percent of Retailers and Brands Will Disappear

We covered the accelerated pursuit among all retailers of private and/or exclusive brands above, primarily to demonstrate that this strategy will provide them greater control over their value chains, allowing them to become small, enclosed "mini-malls." And we touched on the fact that many wholesale brands will be squeezed out of these new models, if not fail altogether.

We also declared that only those retailers and wholesalers that transformed their models to adhere to our three operating principles would survive.

For both these reasons, we predict that 50 percent of all current brands and retailers will disappear.

We cited the growing percentage of private and exclusive brands in the major department and discount store sectors, and our projection that it would reach about 80 percent across retailing. (In Europe, 60 percent of the supermarket shelf space is already occupied by private brands.) We mentioned that Wal-Mart has over 50 percent of its goods as private brands.

In the future, all of retailing will be about narrowing assortments and reducing vendors and wholesale brands, to drive greater control, productivity and profitability. Supervalu announced in 2010 that it would eliminate 25 percent of its current products, and Kroger, 30 percent. Supervalu CEO Craig Herkert stated in a financial-analysts call in February 2010: "The company plans to edit the selection in some categories by as much as 25 percent. The focus is on reducing package sizes rather than entire brands or lines of product, yet in the categories that have already been 'optimized,' some brands have been eliminated completely."[4] And while Kroger was not specific, it is widely known that the chain eliminated 30 percent of the products in its breakfast cereal category, and the results were good—so good that only one item originally cut from the mix was reinstated. It seems that many people cannot get out the door without their bowl of Cap'n Crunch in the morning!

The consumer package goods industry, best exemplified by P&G, has always had a "conflictive collaboration" between its powerhouse brands and retailers' private label goods. Recently, Wal-Mart removed Glad and Hefty brands from its shelves, retaining only one brand, Ziploc. Industry observers expect similar decisions to play out across other categories as the "behemoth from Bentonville" accelerates its effort to simplify brand assortment and focus its support on its Great Value private brand. While the exact selection of products available in Wal-Mart will ebb and flow, the trend is clear. Conversely, P&G, as mentioned before, is testing its own branded, stand-alone stores.

In arts and crafts, both the narrowing of lines and the building of private brands are accelerating. Industry leader Michaels is a great example, with its private Artist's loft brand and the American Girl exclusive branded crafts line. Experts say the drug stores are also getting started, led by Walgreens and CVS. In fact, CVS, in its SKU-cutting strategy, pulled Energizer batteries from the shelves in a bid to simplify choices for consumers. Moreover, Home Depot and Lowe's are beginning to follow suit as well.

Some experts believe that this emphasis on productivity optimization will reduce overall SKU count by more than 15 percent. Kevin Sterneckert, retail research director for AMR Research, believes that retailers are "far from done on the optimization and SKU-reduction fronts."[5]

As for the retail failures we predicted, there have been several over the past few years, among them Steve & Barry's, Bombay, Sharper Image, Levitz, Fortunoff and more. We expect the failures to continue, not because of the recession, but because a growing number of them will not be able to transform their models and positioning in order to provide the elevated experiences we've been defining.

Major challenges are mounting at Kmart and Sears and among the few regional department stores left. The Gap is downsizing its brand and will likely continue, with the jury still out on its turnaround effort. Many small independent retailers who miss the transformation will also fail. We hasten to add, however, that they have the greatest opportunity to outdo big retailers, thanks to their community presence and control over their environment.

For various reasons—the need to control one's supply chain, to increase productivity and profitability, to narrow, downsize and accelerate private branding for differentiation and niche positioning—we conclude that there will be an enormous number of retailers and brands that will not survive into Wave III—50 percent in our estimation.

Demand for Real Value Integrity Is Driving Cost Compression and New Pricing Models

As consumers continue to gain greater knowledge and understanding of what a fair price is for any given product or service relative to its intrinsic value, they are forcing retailers and brands to respond accordingly. For example, consumers more often are less willing to pay a premium for the cachet of a Coach handbag at full price, having discovered one in Costco for half the price, or having found another of similar quality and style in the Coach outlet store, or another brand of like quality in a TJ Maxx off-price store or on any number of online sites.

Putting further pressure on retailers and brands for higher value and lower costs are the new business concepts spawned by such rising consumer intelligence. Fast-fashion retailers, such as Zara, H&M and Forever 21, can view a designer's runway show online, knock-off the style for a much lower cost and have it in its 2000 stores across the world in a matter of weeks. The virtual explosion of private and celebrity brands within department stores provides greater pricing flexibility by not having to share revenues with a wholesale brand. The same holds true for designers' diffusion brands: Vera Wang in Kohl's, Norma Kamali in Wal-Mart, Nicole Miller in JCPenney and many others. The consumer wants the designer cachet, but for a democratically fair price.

Accordingly, the accelerated rollout of outlet stores among brands and retailers (Saks, Bloomingdale's, Nordstrom's, Barney's and others), is a reflection of consumers' pressure for value integrity and lower prices. The growth of members-only luxury sales clubs on the Internet such as Gilt Groupe and Rue La La are also advocates for the new higher-value-for-less consumer. Even in the rapidly share-gaining discount and off-price sectors, they are not just driving lower prices, they are all focusing on providing the highest quality and intrinsic value possible within their sphere.

Finally, the savvy businesses that "get" this new consumer and respond accordingly will force their competitors to follow suit or go out of business. For example, during the Great Recession, Abercrombie & Fitch refused to go on sale in fear of losing or diminishing brand integrity. From 2007 through 2009, revenues decreased roughly 30 percent, a big chunk of it lost to the fierce competitor Aeropostale, which focused on driving a high-value-low-cost strategy.

This consumer price/value quest is not just a recessionary reaction. It is a combination of growing consumer intelligence and businesses' ability to respond. Therefore, it is a long-term trend that will continue to drive whole new business models as well as existing model adaptations.

U.S. Brands, Wholesalers and Retailers Will Be Acquired/Started by Chinese Manufacturers and by Low-Cost Producers

It's interesting that the 150-year history of retailing evolved sequentially in the United States, whereas Waves I, II and III are occurring almost simultaneously in the developing countries around the world, crashing them into the same space the United States inhabits today. This suggests that the transformation of developing countries from production-driven economies into marketing- and consumer-driven economies is almost complete.

Even as these countries continue to benefit from their low-cost production capabilities, they are simultaneously ramping up their marketing and consumption economies, which represents, in some ways, an opportunity for U.S. brands. However, since the world is now "flat," with global markets accessible to all, developing countries would be blind not to recognize vertical integration opportunities in the U.S. marketplace. This is especially true for the Chinese, whose culture has a historically sophisticated understanding of commerce and the profit motive.

On the consumption side, for example, China's average annual household income according to *CIA World Factbook,* was $6,600 in 2009 (a remarkable increase from $3,870 in 2000).[6] In the midst of such rapid growth, their people are hoping to increase their material well-being just as rapidly. India is following a similar path, thought not without significant infrastructural and political barriers that tend to slow their pace.

While many of citizens of India and China, for example, may feel as though they are still in a Wave I, production-driven economy, they can look up from their workbenches and see the massive and rapid growth in infrastructure: vast new distribution and transportation networks; increasing communications; and the formation of markets. Accordingly, this growth applies as well to a retailing infrastructure and industry, which is also witnessing the birth of home-created brands. For example, consider China's Chery automobiles, founded in 1997 and the hugely successful Ports 1961 (launched in that year), luxury fashion line and retail stores, (which it also markets to the United States).[7]

In a sense, China is experiencing the overlap of Waves I and II. And there is even an emerging Wave III, consumption-driven marketplace made up of the country's quickly growing elite. To serve this group, there has been explosive growth in the luxury retailing sector (also benefiting many European and U.S. luxury and fashion brands).

On the business and industrial side, China's rapid growth finds it having amassed an enormous amount of capital, as have other developing countries. Given China's huge capital base, along with the rising incomes of its people, there is no doubt it will continue to barrel forward into Wave III, with a higher standard of living and a consumer market economy. However, peoples' striving for a better standard of living also pushes increased wages, higher taxes, higher energy costs, more infrastructure building, etc. This encapsulates China's economic conflict: it is locked into an ever-increasing standard of living for its people, while at the same time understanding that it cannot afford this standard of living if it wants to remain the low-cost manufacturing base of the world.

China is also feeling global pressure to do just that: maintain low-cost-producer status. That pressure is coming not only from consumer markets around the world, including retailers like Wal-Mart and major brands like Levi's and Nike, but also from within Asia. China's businesses are not only competing among themselves; they also face increasing competition from other low-cost Asian suppliers such as Vietnam, Bangladesh and Indonesia. And, further exacerbating this squeeze, its businesses are currently faced with overcapacity, threatening deflation.

So what's China to do to pull itself out from between the rock and the hard place?

Next Stop: USA

Given China's huge capital position and business acumen, we believe they will proactively address this enormous conundrum. As history's original traders, the Chinese understand better than most where the greatest profits reside on the global value chain—the end closest to the consumer (e.g., retail and brands). And currently, of course, the country with the highest level of profitability, and the most robust markets, brands and retailers, is the United States.

We suggest, then, that China is moving toward a win-win global strategy, with three steps:

1. Identify and acquire U.S. brands and/or retail assets, particularly in those industries that can benefit from vertical integration, such as apparel, where China already produces about 35 percent of all products consumed in the United States. A leading example of this emergent strategy is Li & Fung, the world's largest apparel sourcing agent, at $15 billion. Among sixteen brands it has so far acquired are Emma James, Wear Me, JH Collectibles, Tapemeasure, Regatta, Intuitions, and Rosetti handbags. And China has publicly committed to continuing this strategy, providing vertically integrated control and increasing access to the more profitable U.S. marketplace. From a timing perspective, the iron is hot, as many U.S. brands and retailers have failed or were weakened during the recession.

    And though the apparel industry may be low-hanging fruit, we believe that China will leverage its experience in that sector to examine every industry, with an ultimate focus on the retail end of the chain.

    So, instead of continuing to buy U.S. Treasury bills, China will be buying assets. As stated in the April 6, 2010 issue of the *Wall Street Journal,* between 2002 and 2008, China's direct investment in the United States increased more than threefold, to $1.3 billion, according to the Bureau of Economic Analysis.[8] Initially, however, the Chinese companies will likely keep U.S. management in place, due to their lack of marketing and distribution skills in this country.

This assures us that the important creative, innovative and entrepreneurial skills so unique to the United States will remain essential. Those people will simply be reporting to a different owner.

2. Vertical integration not only provides China greater profits, thus fueling its rapidly growing economy and standard of living, it provides total control over both its value chains and their markets. For example, China would be the major consumer market for its own products, and would have the power to put pressure on all its former low-cost competitors, for even lower costs. With ownership of globally recognized brands, and total control of its value chains, China can market them at home as well as throughout the world.

3. On the other hand, there is strong evidence that another prong of the strategy for China and other developing countries revolves around their homegrown entrepreneurs and innovators.

    As the *Economist* pointed out on April 17, 2010: "The world's creative energy is shifting to the developing countries, which are becoming innovators in their own right rather than just talented imitators. . . . Even more striking is the emerging world's growing ability to make established products for dramatically lower costs: no-frills $3000 cars and $300 laptops may not seem as exciting as a new iPad but they promise to change far more people's lives. The sort of advance—dubbed 'frugal innovation' by some—is not just a matter of exploiting cheap labor (though cheap labor helps). It is a matter of redesigning products and processes to cut out unnecessary costs."[9]

Moreover, as these countries continue to grow, they will be developing their own brands, particularly for their mass markets. Big, globally recognized U.S. brands may thus lose at least some of their luster over time. The *Economist* continues: "The winners in these markets will not be big (global) brands that will not be relevant to the mass market." They will be Chinese or Indian brands. Even now that trend is visible. To quote the April 17, 2010 issue of the *Economist* again: "Black & Decker, America's biggest toolmaker, is almost invisible in India and China, the world's two biggest construction sites."

Soon enough, then, there will be a twofold and globally disruptive dynamic occurring among the developing countries: first, the acquisition of U.S. (and other) marketplace assets (brands and retailers), and with it the power of a totally controlled (actually owned) value chain; and second, the continuing development of their own markets, including innovation and creation of their own brands and retail businesses. Former investment banker Felix Rohatyn was quoted in the April 13, 2010 issue of the *Wall Street Journal* in an article titled: "Lazard's Statesman, a Game-Changer": "Control will go with capital."[10] And today, of course, China controls a massive amount of the world's capital.

Finally, since innovation is best executed by those who control the value from creation through distribution and interaction with the consumer, we believe there will also be new brands innovated in the developing countries to be marketed in the United States.

One historic example is Japan's contribution to innovation in the automobile industry, which turned the U.S. market on its head. They not only created smaller fuel-efficient cars while the United States stuck to "gas-guzzlers" during the OPEC oil crisis and skyrocketing gas prices during the 1970s, but they also innovated quality control standards and processes that produced cars that were initially far superior to American made automobiles. Certainly the same potential for these developing countries exists across multiple retail and consumer businesses in the United States. Let's look at how we would compete in this environment.

Many companies, like VF Corporation and P&G, already see this challenge and have built a clear global competency in all elements of the value chain. Investing in a flexible value chain not only supports the complex and highly segmented markets in the United States but also enables them to meet the unique demands of the new and developing markets.

Other companies might choose to become "masters of frugal innovation" for the developing world, innovating affordable new products and services specifically for those countries. For example, Unilever has opened its concept center in Shanghai to conduct day to day research on the Chinese consumer. Proctor & Gamble is doing the same. Perhaps the current poster child is Nokia with inexpensive phones for almost every income strata in Asia.

And there remains one possible area of competitive advantage that could be exportable: "experience" innovation, or our superiority in marketing and creating experiential branding and the shopping experience. What we have been discussing as an imperative for U.S. brands will soon become even more crucial in the developing world. Indeed, survival into Wave III requires a global presence one way or another.

Although this may seem like a dire scenario for the United States, we do not believe all our great brands and/or retailers will be acquired by developing countries. In fact, we believe just as strongly that another of our predictions will more than offset our asset losses in that direction. As a nation of entrepreneurs, and with consumers desiring ever more customization, localization, niche brands and so forth, we predict the continual emergence of an infinite number of finite markets, served by an infinite number of finite or niche brands and/or services, distributed on an infinite number of distribution platforms. And because of their smaller size, resulting in tighter and more responsive value chains, much of the development and production of those brands and services will be domestic.

The Transformation of Communications, Advertising and Media Business Models

Just as retail, wholesale and service business models are being driven by consumers in saturated markets, these same dynamics are driving an equally fundamental transformation in the communications, advertising and media industries.

This matters because marketing occupies a critical part of the value chain. Without its effective implementation, the achievement of the neurological connection will be impeded, and preemptive distribution is enhanced when it is effectively led by communications and advertising.

So, along with consumer behavioral shifts, technological advances continue to expand an infinite number of distribution platforms for communications, products and services that can literally follow and access individual consumers 24/7. Unfortunately for marketers, the same technological innovations have allowed the consumer to not only block what they do not want entering their "space," but also to invite or grant permission to precisely what they would welcome.

What this means is that communication about products or services is no longer controlled by the company. The power of social network sites, blogs and other electronic platforms is that they more than counterbalance the traditionally well-orchestrated marketing messages from the consumer products businesses. For instance, Pampers' launch of Dry Max diaper in 2010 was substantially hindered by online critics; an article in the *Financial Times* referred to the diaper and the online contagion by saying, "The criticism . . . spread like a rash."[11]

Hence a fundamental transformation of the media and advertising industries to finitely target both content and distribution, where they can measure quality and cost of contact. VF Corporation has described this future; it envisions defining and measuring its millions of consumers as "universes of one."

In addition to the overabundance of stores, stuff and everything else over the past twenty years, there has also been a deluge of communication of all types, including advertising, accommodated by the equally enormous deluge of media and communications platforms (most notably, of course, the Internet).

With over 50 billion websites emitting enough information to fill seventeen Libraries of Congress every three years, hundreds of TV channels (compared to a handful in Wave II), enough magazine titles to accommodate every niche interest and many, many more communications platforms, all chasing after every single consumer and bombarding them with noise, consumers have finally said, "No more."

The collective switches of the marketplace went from "on" to "off" several years ago. And traditional media and the advertising world are just now, glacially, attempting to convert their antiquated approaches into models that seek an invitation into consumers' lives.

As in retailing, short of a total overhaul, consumers will continue to turn off when confronted by advertising content and media overload. Remember, it is the consumer who switches your lights on in the morning, and who can switch them off for good anytime, for any reason.

Viewership, readership and listenership have shifted, and continue to shift, from TV, magazines, newspapers and radio to the Internet. This is also where consumers can find most content free or almost free, and where they can pull out what they choose, rather than having ads and information pushed at them. It's also interactive in real time, for immediate gratification. As a consequence, all the ratings measures of the traditional media, along with all their top and bottom lines, plummeted in the 2000s, and continue downward today.

Traditional media and advertising, like traditional retailing, must transform themselves to be responsive to the very same consumer shifts that are transforming all consumer-facing industries. Otherwise they, too, will disappear. Many already have.

P&G got it. As early as February 2, 2004, in a *Forbes.com* article by Melanie Wells, its global marketing officer James Stengel said: "The mass-marketing model is dead. This (word of mouth) is the future."[12]

Putting its money where its mouth was, P&G launched the Tremor Division, consisting of 280,000 teenagers (1 percent of the 13- to 19-year-old population in the United States at the time) who, for nothing more than a few coupons and product samples, spread the word (and samples), endorsing the products at school, at parties and sleepovers, by cell phone and email. And at the time only a third of Tremor's activities were devoted to P&G products. Most of the information spreading was for other national brands such as AOL, Coca-Cola, Kraft Foods and Toyota, for which P&G charged hefty fees.

Such word-of-mouth young marketers are in great demand across all consumer-facing industries, given their dexterity with the plethora of social networks and unlimited interactive devices.

What's Next?

So what is the future going to hold for advertising, marketing and media? How are they going to transform their models to survive and serve the twenty-first-century consumer?

David Kirkpatrick, a senior editor and columnist for *Fortune* magazine, referring to the book *The Future of Competition: Co-Creating Unique Value with Customers,* not only reinforced our thesis regarding retailing's transformation, but also provided a new framework for us to theorize about the future of media and advertising. He said we're entering a "bottom-up-economy," one in which consumers will migrate to businesses that allow them to be participants in the process of creating what they want. There are no better examples of this today than YouTube, Hulu, and Facebook, which is projected to soon have 1.6 billion new friends, with 1 billion in Asia.[13]

Permission and Co-creation

Future consumers are going to be "wired," but only to what they choose to be wired to. Consumers will construct their own life model, essentially a file of all those things they like or want—products, services, brands, books, magazines, entertainment, etc. They will key in those things that will be "permitted" entry into their space. Conversely, there will be an explicit list of what they will not permit, as well as instructions as to when and how they want to be reached. All consumer businesses will have access to that file.

Consider this scenario: A male consumer is shaving in the morning, listening to a voice emanating from his personalized global communications center, an audio stream of information that he has permitted while shaving every morning. He has been driving a BMW for two years. The voice reminds him of the mileage he has accumulated and then informs him there are two great new models he might like to check out. Mercedes Benz has also been permitted into this space, and it, too, describes its newest models. The messages are totally informational, with no marketing hype.

That evening, as he's watching a documentary on his favorite sport, car racing, he taps a pause button to permit a three-minute "infotainment" segment, a hyped-up, Hollywood-level piece, dramatizing the performance of the new Porsche, all with special effects, music and so forth.

His entire working, social and leisure life is peppered with this form of customized, controlled and permitted communications, through all mediums.

In this new communications model, businesses will be permitted to enter the consumer's life only with messages that are factual, informative, educational or entertaining, and only those customized to the individual's needs, wants and lifestyle. And all will be delivered when, how, where and for the duration permitted by the individual, as specified in their "life" file.

Perhaps the greatest impact of this new communications model will be felt by the media industry. In this scenario, advertising will no longer subsidize media. Like everything else in the future, the content and programming of print, broadcast or online media must have its own intrinsic value for those consumers the medium is targeting. Consumers will determine its value and will pay a fair price for that value.

The good news for all marketers in this projected future is that they will be able to communicate directly and precisely with their existing and targeted consumers more efficiently and effectively, and with very quantifiable measures of return on investment. Revolutions are painful and costly, but considerably less so than consumers putting you out of business.

PART 3

THE MASTERS

CHAPTER 9

THE MASTER MODEL

APPAREL RETAIL SPECIALTY CHAINS

Since its inception in the 1960s, the branded-apparel retail chain sector, which includes J. Crew, Aeropostale, Gap and many others, has grown faster than any other retail channel. While there are many variables for the relative success or failure of any one of these branded chains, in the aggregate, the reason for their tremendous success in gobbling up share from their competitors, and particularly the department stores, is the strategic foundation of their model. Its entire focus is on connecting with their consumer neurologically, ensuring them quickest and easiest access to their customers (preemptive distribution). And because the brand name on the door is the same as all the merchandise in the store, they have total control over their value chain, particularly those functions that "touch" the consumer, both in getting direct input from them (the co-creation of their desires) and the final connection at the point-of-sale. It is this totally controlled value chain that enables the neurological connection and preemptive access in the first place.

Let's examine some of the inherent advantages of this model, based on our three operating principles: neurological connectivity, preemptive distribution and value-chain control.

Neurological Connectivity

Better Potential for Creating the Neurological Connection

Because the entire presentation and environment are devoted to one brand, and the entirety of its imagery is consistent, these specialty chains can more easily create the desired experience. Tommy Bahama's "resort" area retail format provides a laid-back island resort atmosphere, including a bar and restaurant with live music as well as a themed apparel area. Chico's creates an intimate, clubby environment involving a great deal of interaction between the customers and the associates. A communal mirror forces customers out of the dressing rooms, giving sales associates an opportunity to tell them how great they look, and also to suggest coordinating accessories and other items. Many other chains employ similar lifestyle experiences.

Because of these neurological experiences, consumers will pay more, stay longer, return first to the store (thus preempting competitors), will come back more often and will remain loyal longer.

More Intimate and Easier Shopping Experience

Most of the specialty chains occupy 3500–5000 square feet. This provides a smaller, casual, more intimate and less frustrating shopping environment than department-store models. Therefore, the specialty chain model accommodates either a personalized, relaxed shopping experience or a quick in-and-out if the customer so desires.

Single Dedicated Space for Cohesive and
Total Lifestyle Presentation

Since all their space is devoted to one branded lifestyle, specialty chains can present their total lifestyle concept, including all the products representing it, in one place. Conversely, many lifestyle brands carried in department and traditional stores find their various product categories spread throughout multiple departments and on different floors. The specialty model also allows the presentation of a broader mix of products and deeper, better-edited assortments.

More Focused, Knowledgeable and Effective Associates

This focused model simplifies the hiring, training and retention of sales associates. In fact, most specialty chains hire associates who match the profile of their core consumer. Abercrombie & Fitch, Charming Shoppes, Chico's and many others staff their stores in this manner. In fact, the majority of Chico's and other chains' associates were hired directly from their consumer bases. Obviously, the learning curve for these associates is shortened because of their familiarity with the products, the service and the whole shopping experience. They can immediately relate to the customers, and because they already love the brand, they find it easier to share that love when they're working as associates. For all these reasons, associates' turnover is lower in the specialty sector. For example, Chico's turnover is about 50 percent annually, compared to the industry norm of 75 percent.

Provides Real-Time Research and Relationship Building

Finally, since the consumers are essentially stepping into the brand when they step into the store, there are no competing brand distractions. Customers are captive. This provides an opportunity for the associates to do real-time research to determine what's hot and what's not, and most important, whether their customers are satisfied (and if not, why not). In many cases, moreover, the associates will become friendly enough with their loyal customer base that they interact with them freely about the arrival of special new products, sending birthday cards, wishing them well and so forth.

In fact, in some cases, such as Mitchell's men's store in Westport, Connecticut, it is company policy.

Preemptive Distribution

Smaller Flexible Footprints for More Accessible Locations

Thanks to a single consumer and lifestyle focus and smaller footprints, specialty chains have maximum potential for moving their stores farther into the consumers' neighborhoods, providing even more convenience. And while many of them, such as the Gap or A&F, are currently mall based, as mall traffic declines, replaced by the faster-growing lifestyle neighborhood shopping centers, these brands will also move. Many of them, like Charming Shoppes, are already going off-mall for all new store openings.

Neurologically Defined Experience as Preemptive Destination

They are *the* brand; therefore, the entire store and everything in it is *the* destination, including the neurological experience. This is much more effective than having a single brand or product category located within the complex maze of stuff housed in the departmental models. This element also enables the brand to develop and present itself more quickly, clearly and cohesively on all possible distribution platforms, both offline and online.

Value-Chain Control

Ownership of One Integrated Supply Chain Makes Possible the Neurological Connection, Preemptive Distribution and Therefore the Overall Superior Value

Since they use a consumer-direct model, specialty chains have maximum control, if not outright ownership, of their entire supply chains from creation through consumption. This is what makes the neurological connection and preemptive distribution possible. It also affords maximum efficiency, flexibility, reduced cycle times for more new lines, localizing the product offerings, and control over inventory and excesses, all without the time, complexity and compromise that comes with a multiplicity of vendors and/or suppliers.

Single Lifestyle and Consumer Focus

The specialty chain model focuses on a lifestyle, and typically on one product category and consumer segment. Structurally and operationally, therefore, it is much less complex than stores serving multimarket segments. As a result, concentrated strategy and execution provide the consumer with a fuller, more satisfying shopping experience, including a more specialized and intelligently edited product assortment.

Inherent Tactical Disadvantages

While the strategic advantages of the specialty retail model are far more enduring and critical than any tactical disadvantages, the disadvantages are nonetheless worth noting because they can cause serious setbacks to the business and erode brand strength.

This scenario is best exemplified by the Gap's near-death experience and Ann Taylor's downward spiral during the early 2000s. If these chains "miss" on product styling for a season, the miss gets negatively leveraged across their entire chains, just as their "hits" leveraged their meteoric growth. Miss two or more consecutive seasons, and enormous revenue losses can turn into the more dangerous condition of consumers' turning away from the brand altogether. Certainly, in today's world, those disappointed consumers have an unlimited number of equivalent, if not superior, shopping choices to select from. Traditional retail models, on the other hand, spread the risk of such mistakes across a multitude of brands. If one brand misses, there are many others that can make up for it.

Further exacerbating this challenge for specialty chains is their tendency to become insular and lose touch with the broader fashion marketplace, which is where ideas, trends, and innovative new fabrics are discussed among various industry constituencies.

On balance, however, the specialty chain sectors' growth rate and number-one share position confirm that their advantages far outweigh their weaknesses. And most important, because they are strategically best positioned among all competitors, they can correct tactical errors of execution and still recover—as the Gap and Ann Taylor appear to be doing now by repositioning their merchandise styling and mix, and improving the shopping experience.

Approaching a New Paradigm in Specialty Retailing

A new truth universally acknowledged in the specialty sector is that the days of the mega-brand—one brand covering all product categories and consumer segments—are over.

Indeed, the paradigm is shifting in favor of an infinite number of finitely segmented consumer niches, being served by an infinite array of finitely focused brands.

We've mentioned previously some examples of this paradigm shift: A&F's spinning off the Hollister and Abercrombie branded chains, targeting different consumer niches; Chico's acquiring White House/Black Market and launching Soma Intimates; Urban Outfitters with its Free People and Anthropologie offshoots, all three positioned to target different consumer segments, with different lifestyles and shopping experiences; and J. Crew launching Crewcuts for Kids and Madewell for boomers.

But why is this new paradigm evolving?

It is the result of three dynamics working in tandem:

- Because of unlimited selection, consumers are seeking exclusivity. They want things that are special, just for them. Mass markets are in decline.
- The consumers' ability to achieve exclusivity is being enabled by an infinitely fragmented and dispersed media and marketing infrastructure, including the explosion of new channels of distribution.
- Technology is further enabling the consumers' demands for exclusivity. Superior information, logistics and distribution technologies are elevating supply-chain capabilities to support multiple market and brand segments and smaller exclusive niches, including different line mixes according to geographic preferences.

The Model to Beat or Imitate

Based on the strength of this retail model and the share dominance in apparel it has achieved, primarily taken from the department-store sector, one could argue that some of the major department stores are fighting back with the same weaponry used against them.

For example, there is no question that Macy's, Bloomingdale's, JCPenney, Kohl's and regional player Belk are all focused on elevating their respective shopping experiences (friendlier, more attentive associates, better lighting, less clutter for quick and easy scanning of the entire store, greater use of mannequin displays for outfit suggestions, smaller vignettes, music, videos and colorful graphics, cooking and other classes, restaurants, celebrity and designer fashion shows, etc.). Again, the neuroexperience achieved in each case will be different, consistent with its brand image and customer expectations.

As we already suggested, if the experience is strong enough, those stores will preemptively get their customers back to their stores before they go to a competitor. Beyond this, they participate on all distribution platforms, including staking out a presence in the social networks such as Facebook, Twitter, etc.

As predicted, and as some are already doing, they will roll out smaller neighborhood store formats, as JCPenney and Bloomingdale's have done, for both preemptive distribution and localizing the product mix and experience. We also predict a direct attack on the specialists by the department stores rolling out their own private brands into the specialty chain format (e.g., Alfani, Stafford or Arizona specialty chains).

Finally, as we argued earlier, their pursuit of ever-more-private and exclusive brands will eventually give department stores even greater control over their entire value chains.

We believe that this is the kind of transformation traditional department stores must make to survive. More optimistically, if they do it right, they have the potential to claw back much of their lost apparel share. Furthermore, the model we predict for the winners will have an advantage over the specialists, thanks to the greater breadth of their product and experiential offerings.

Indeed, it would be a great irony if the department stores pulled a "back to the future" and once again became the palaces of consumption they were known as at the beginning of Wave I.

CHAPTER 10

IDEAS FROM THE MASTERS

WHOLESALERS, RETAILERS OR BRAND MANAGERS?

Following are some selections we made of retailers and wholesalers that developed some differentiated applications of one or all three of our strategic operating principles. We felt not only that they would support our thesis, but that they may very well provide applicable ideas for all businesses.

VF Corporation

VF Corporation is the largest apparel company in the United States, with almost $8 billion in annual revenues. While not known as a retailer, it is one of the best examples of a wholesaler executing our three imperative strategies in tandem with the three-wave history of the retail industry as described in this book. Founded in Wave I, VF was a production-driven, wholesale apparel company with one brand (Vanity Fair intimate apparel), distributed solely in the United States through department stores. Today, it is a marketing-driven wholesaler and retailer with a portfolio of over thirty brands and sub-brands, and it has expanded distribution through all channels, including its own retail stores and the global marketplace (from 2001 to 2008, international sales grew from 19 percent to 30 percent of revenues). VF's stable of brands includes Wrangler, Lee, Seven For All Mankind, The North Face, Kipling, Vans, Reef, Jansport and Nautica, among others.

Consumer Responsiveness and Value-Chain Control

VF's evolution toward our three operating principles has been timely and steady. In the 1980s VF realized the impact that consumer power and its changing demands were going to have on its business. Accordingly, it began to change its strategic direction and business model. It launched a major, company-wide initiative to become a leader in consumer responsiveness. Attached to that goal was the need for a totally integrated, highly collaborative value chain—one that it could totally control.

At the time, VF owned the manufacturing of its two major brands: Lee Jeans and Vanity Fair Intimates. By the mid-1980s, it had added Wrangler, Jantzen and Jansport, ensuring control of that end of the value chain. However, VF also realized that a paradigm shift was occurring that could not be ignored. Manufacturing was seeking the lowest cost possible to stay price competitive in the heated battle for consumers. Thus all manufacturing in the textile and apparel industries inevitably started to move to Mexico, Central and South America and especially Asia.

Understanding the vital link between their goal of total responsiveness to consumers and the need for the entire value chain to support that goal, VF realized it had to manage what would become a totally outsourced function in the chain.

VF's early understanding of this game-changing combination of events helped it focus on strategically adapting, internally and externally. Let's examine the process.

Consumers: From Single-Product Brands to Lifestyle Brands

First, VF's consumer-responsiveness process, based on what is arguably the most sophisticated consumer research and tracking process in its industry, identified the trend of consumers seeking so-called lifestyle brands (e.g., Ralph Lauren and Abercrombie & Fitch) over single-product category brands like its heritage brands, Lee jeans and Vanity Fair intimates. This sparked an aggressive acquisition strategy, manifested in the 2004 launch of its plan to transform VF into a global lifestyle apparel company with a high-growth portfolio of lifestyle brands such as The North Face, Seven for All Mankind and the others we've mentioned.

In 2000, VF's heritage brands accounted for 90 percent of revenues. By 2008, however, that number dropped to 56 percent, with lifestyle brands reaching 44 percent of total sales. Management predicted that lifestyle brands would generate 60 percent of revenues from 2007 onward.

Mackey McDonald, a former VF CEO who spearheaded the early stages of VF's huge transformation in the 1990s, later commented in 2007 on VF's response to shifting consumer desires. His point was that VF identified a trend that consumers were buying fewer items, but spending more for each. This indicated they wanted to make a stronger statement about the brands they wore along with the particular lifestyles they lived.

Value-Chain Control: From Vertical Control to Managed and Controlled Collaborations

The expertise gained from VF's original vertically owned manufacturing served it well as it transitioned to the necessary collaborations with manufacturers and suppliers around the world.

During its early stages, offshore sourcing went to the lowest-cost countries. But because of VF's commitment to consumer responsiveness as the driving force in the value chain, it was quick to

understand that the "lowest cost" was not enough of a differentiator. It evaluated the other aspects it considered important, such as
speed to market, better material utilization, lower inventories, less
work in progress and lower cost to quality. While lower price was,
naturally, still high on consumers' lists, they had raised the bar.
Low prices were just the price of entry.

As conceptualized by a VF supply chain executive, reducing
the amount of "needle time" that applies to making a garment is no
longer a competitive advantage. It's about managing the entire supply chain, and this is where he felt VF was excelling and gaining
great advantage over competitors.

Accordingly, VF came up with its Third Way sourcing strategy, a hybrid of complete supply-chain control and relationships
with suppliers. The Third Way helped reduce costs and lower inventory while increasing productivity and better integrating ac-
quisitions. It also gave VF maximum control over the supply chain.
Here's how it worked:

- VF would strike an agreement with a supplier for a specific
  product line (e.g., backpacks) and commit to a volume fore-
  cast over a number of years (instead of one season). The
  supplier would agree not to produce the same category of
  product (e.g., backpacks) for competitors going forward.
- The supplier would set up production lines dedicated to
  VF's products, investing in the building, machinery, equipment, labor supervision, logistics services and administrative infrastructure to manage the operations.
- VF and the supplier would develop production schedules
  jointly to meet each partner's needs. Information on order
  forecasts and production capacity was to be shared between
  the partners.
- VF and the supplier would work together on process improvements. VF would make available (without charge) its
  engineering resources to improve production processes. A

portion of the savings realized by these improvements would be passed through to VF.

- The supplier would own the factory and the equipment and be responsible for managing the workforce. VF would make certain investments in specialized equipment and capital when necessary.

- VF would use its purchasing capacity to help the suppliers procure fabric and other raw materials at discounted prices. VF would agree to buy back any unused fabric or raw material from the supplier.

Based on all of the above and more, VF has the most advanced, efficient, technologically superior and best-managed supply chain in its industry.

As former CEO Mackey McDonald has expressed on many occasions throughout his tenure, VF's supply chain management has been a "competitive weapon" for many years. And he has clearly stressed the importance of maintaining that advantage. Certainly, current CEO Eric Wiseman is doing exactly that. In a phone conversation in May 2010, he responded to the industries' prevalent use of third-party sourcing agents by pointing out that if VF felt sourcing agents could "do a better job managing and controlling that part of our business, we would use them. We believe we do all of it better."[1]

Furthermore, the structure of VF's portfolio provides an inherent synergy between the front and back ends of the business. The front end consists of its multiplicity of brands, all decentralized. Each is autonomous, run by its own management, tasked with maintaining the brand's integrity, entrepreneurial culture and its focus and connectivity with its core consumers. Meanwhile, the back end is centralized (with the corporate experts using the efficiencies and productivity afforded by scale), and is able to support the front end's all-important need to be consumer responsive.

Preemptive Distribution and Neurological Connection:
Each Brand's Role

As we mentioned, VF's lifestyle brands currently account for 44 percent of total sales. However, they are the fastest-growing segment of the business, and VF's stated goal is to continue acquiring lifestyle brands. More important, it seeks only those brands that also have a retail component, since they expect this retail, "direct-to-consumer" business across all brands to grow faster than its wholesale business.

Mentioned several times throughout the book, CEO Eric Wiseman has declared that "[retail] will grow much more dramatically than our overall growth rate. In lifestyle brands like Vans, The North Face, and Nautica, we want to continue to present the brand in ways we can control."[2] In 2007 he projected that "by 2012 international revenues will comprise a third of total revenues, while our direct-to-consumer business will account for 22% of total revenues, and we aim to hit $11 billion in total revenues."[3]

Currently, with about 700 single-brand stores, VF plans to open 75 to 100 stores each year, to reach 1300 stores globally by 2012. Many of these stores are planned for Asia.

While this goal suggests an intention to increase control over its distribution, VF's decentralized business model requires that strategic decision-making on all consumer-touching points in the value chain be made at the brand level. For example, all The North Face consumer research, brand positioning, marketing, advertising, brand imagery, distribution and creation of the brand experience are the responsibilities of The North Face management team alone. This applies across VF's entire portfolio of brands.

However, consistent with VF's strategic growth strategy, the common thread that runs through all its brands is the use of all relevant distribution platforms (online and off), in pursuit of a strategy of preemptively reaching its consumers ahead of the competition. And since most of its lifestyle brands, like The North Face, control their retail component, they also control the brand experience and the neurological connection with the consumer. In fact, even when those brands, along with VF's wholesale brands such as Wrangler and Lee jeans, distribute through retailers like Wal-Mart, Kohl's, JCPenney, Macy's and others, they insist on a strong collaboration to ensure their brands' appropriate merchandising, presentation and strategic integrity. Industry experts have explained VF's strength in its retail partnerships as springing from its deep consumer knowledge, coupled with its superior supply-chain control and rapid responsiveness. To reiterate one of the most illustrative examples, VF is able to distribute two different line mixes of Wrangler jeans to two different Wal-Mart stores that may be just across town from each other.

Concerning its strategic evolution toward distribution control, VF's website states: "With over 700 retail stores, we understand the importance of creating a unique environment that allows us to directly communicate the excitement of our brands to consumers. Growing our base of branded retail stores will be an important part of our strategy. We are also expanding our e-commerce capabilities via our brand websites to provide consumers greater access to our products."[4]

The North Face

With its mantra and tagline, "Never Stop Exploring," The North Face is a premier active outdoor brand, promising authenticity and unparalleled performance benefits in its apparel and equipment products for climbing/hiking, biking, running, skiing, snowboarding, trekking/travel and training. Its core consumers are men, women and kids who pursue those outdoor activities, as well as sophisticated urbanites.

Ever since its bankruptcy in 2000, The North Face has successfully revamped its strategic operations, with impressive results.

The North Face has grown threefold between 2003 and 2010 to $2.4 billion, and consistently delivers 14 percent profit margins. It has become the cornerstone of VF Corporation's Outdoor and Sportswear Coalition.

The turnaround at The North Face has been built upon the synergy of all three of our strategic operating principles.

Like all great sports brands, The North Face is continuously adding genuine athletes from each of its outdoor activities to its "team" (currently up to sixty members) in order to provide feedback, and consulting with outside design companies with expertise in biomechanics and performance. Essentially, these athletes are consumer advocates and continually build on the authenticity and performance of the brand. Most important are the innovations that emanate from the teams: True to its performance positioning, The North Face focuses on technology innovations like "Hyvent," waterproof breathable polyurethane coatings and moisture-wicking "Vaporwick" fabric. And recently its Single-Track running shoe won a Best Debut award from *Runner's World* for its innovations in superior technology, design and performance.

The North Face also sponsors over forty athletes a year and as many as ten expeditions annually to maintain the brand's exposure to its core customers. It also leverages abundant and available video footage of the athletes wearing The North Face products to engage the customers.

However, regardless of how well The North Face implements such a strategy, it is not unique. Other major sports brands pursue similar programs. We believe the real key to the successful turnaround was its ability to leverage the superior value chain of its parent, VF Corporation (which acquired the brand in 2000). For example, when VF took over, it merged The North Face into its network of factories in Asia and what is now an 1,100-person procurement office in Hong Kong. The North Face went from shipping half the orders on time to over 90 percent on time. And not only did this corporate synergy improve its more basic operational effectiveness, but it also facilitated the expansion of the in-store experience (neurological connectivity) and preemptive distribution.

As it increased their store base (currently over fifty stores), The North Face also began enhancing the experience. Digital kiosks were put into the stores to both entertain and show the actual products in action. Moreover, the videos were capable of showing many more products than could be stocked in the store, but which could be ordered online. An ancillary benefit of the digital kiosk, incidentally, is its ability to efficiently train salespeople.

The store environment and presentation were also designed to connect with the customers' sense of being enveloped by the "real experiences" of their chosen sport, and in addition to the videos there are large visual graphics. As the company opened stores, in some cases it did so close to its wholesale partners (such as department stores that carry the line). And, contrary to some experts' long-held beliefs that they would cannibalize each other's business or fall into pricing conflicts, neither happened. In fact, sales rose in both locations. In London, The North Face opened a store in the same vicinity as its largest distributor store. The excitement generated in The North Face store led to more products being carried in the store across the street, and to greater sales for both. This exemplifies the power of both the in-store experience and preemptive distribution.

Another unique application of the preemptive distribution strategy and providing a special, perceived custom product is The North Face's clever use of mobile electronics as a marketing tool. For example, a North Face loyalist who happens to be within a two-mile radius of one of its stores might receive a text message informing him of a new backpack that's just arrived, with a special offer just for him.

All these examples are a result of The North Face's use of its parent's well-executed and highly controlled value chain.

The key challenge for The North Face is to be able to work with the VF corporate team and maintain its own production process that is "demand-pull" driven based on consumers actual purchases (as opposed to "forecasting-push" driven, projecting what the company believes will be purchased), and to remain both flexible and responsive to its ever-evolving consumer demands and the experience they expect. With multiple businesses to support, the VF value chain will also need to continue to evolve its flexibility to support these individual business requirements.

Best Buy

At first, Best Buy would seem to be the classic department store within the electronics sector. Everything is merchandised by category and grouped by brand—almost identical to the traditional department store model. In fact, with strong "power brands" (e.g., Sony, Nintendo, Canon, etc.), it might seem that Best Buy would be subject to the same operational weaknesses and competitive threats as the traditional department stores. Just one example would be online competitors' selling the same brands carried by Best Buy for a lower price. However, Best Buy is deploying all three of our strategic principles, thereby clearly differentiating its stores from all competitors.

For example, it has organized its entire model and all its strategies to experientially engage and exceed the expectations of every one of its customers, to the point of customizing for them. Best Buy wants to be a must-go-to-first destination, where customers know not only that they are going to find things that are special for them, but that it's going to be a relaxed, educational and fun experience.

In fact, a recent $50 million renovation of 110 stores was designed around five core consumer groups that Best Buy has identified:

1. For "Jill," the suburban busy mother, it created an easily traversed store layout, and included technology-related toys

for children. It also added personal shopping assistants to educate these mostly technophobic customers. Finally, more of the floor space is allocated to household appliances.

2. "Buzz" is a technology junkie for whom stores are loaded with interactive displays for trying out new equipment and media.

3. "Barry," an affluent, time-pressed yuppie seeking pricier products and more service, will find his Best Buy store tailored for him, with things such as pricey home theater setups.

4. "Ray," who has a family on a budget, will find more moderately priced merchandise, financing plans and loyalty programs.

5. Small business customers are catered to with specially trained staffs, office equipment and even mobile service technicians they call "Geek Squads."[5]

Best Buy used various data, including demographic, lifestyle and marketplace data, to identify the critical factors driving sales in each store location. Customized training of sales associates and the Geek Squads was conducted to provide the different service required from each group. And store layouts, presentation and, of course, line mixes were localized as well. As a result of this effort, reported same-store sales growth for the remodeled customer-centric stores exceeded 9 percent. This figure was double the same-store sales growth for outlets that were not converted.

Whether browsing for electronic gadgets, comparing computers or TV sets, customers know they will receive guidance, and even Geek Squad service support following the purchase. Best Buy also provides a continual stream of new and relevant products, based on their customer knowledge. For example, it offered Apple's newest product, the iPad, immediately following its release in 2010.

The Geek Squad is perhaps the greatest differentiator and competitive advantage uniquely "owned" by Best Buy. With 24,000

Geeks worldwide, coming to work in a uniform of white button-down shirts, black pants and clip-on ties, and making house calls in black-and-white "Geekmobiles," Best Buy views them as its "killer app." And now Wal-Mart, Target, Sam's Club and Costco are trying to duplicate them.

Beyond the Geek Squad, Best Buy also provides installation, tech support and warranties to its consumers. By providing this full-service experience to its customers, Best Buy sends the message that the purchase of a gadget or electronic device is more than a transaction. It is the informed process leading up to, and the guaranteed retailer support following, the acquisition of that product.

Finally, Best Buy connects with its consumers' sense of "community" and all things green. It has a massive recycling program. Since it began a program offering free recycling of gadgets, more than 25 million pounds of goods have been turned in, growing at sixty products a day. Best Buy is America's biggest collector of electronic garbage. It began to focus on the environment at the request of its workers and customers. The customers' message was that they preferred doing business with retailers that cared about their community.

In addition to gaining preemptive distribution through the localization of each of its stores, Best Buy is also rolling out over a hundred smaller neighborhood stores of 3500–5000 square feet. They have different nameplates, different store formats, layouts, presentations, product offerings and levels of service, according to the consumer preferences and needs in each neighborhood. For example, in a yuppie neighborhood, the service and products would be different from those required in a boomer neighborhood. In one of the most challenging retail sectors, electronics, Best Buy is trying to establish a tight neurological connection with its consumers that trumps other distribution platforms.

It is also expanding the opening of one thousand Best Buy Mobile stores, selling cell phones and mobile electronics.

Of course, Best Buy is integrated across all distribution platforms and with great sophistication, given its electronics expertise. Furthermore, it is preemptively distributing by partnering with third-party vendors to create innovative products and services. For example, to beef up the sales of TVs and DVD players, constantly advancing, multiple-model markets, Best Buy partnered with Netflix, the national video provider, and developed for its premier customers its Blue Sky Video by Best Buy free movie rental download program. It also offers streaming service to customers who purchase Insignia DVD players. Combining two products that customers would otherwise need to search for in different locations to obtain, Best Buy is able to preemptively distribute its offerings.

Finally, to preemptively distribute on the grander, global scale, Best Buy has turned to the international market to help boost its sales and market penetration. In recent years, it has expanded its operations to Mexico, the United Kingdom, Turkey and most recently China. As of this writing, there are planned openings for fifteen stores in China.

Since Best Buy has multiple vendors and suppliers throughout the world with whom it must closely collaborate, it's a difficult challenge to have total control over the operation of its value chain. However, their CEO, Brian Dunn, quite strongly declares the one part of the chain they do own: "While Wal-Mart outsources 'house calls' to service customers to a company named NEW, based in Virginia, Best Buy owns the Geek Squads. The operative word here is owns. Outsourcing works for back office operations, but we believe that when an experience touches a customer, you must own it."[6]

In accordance with that logic, Best Buy is also developing private-label and exclusive products in key categories and investing in the in-store experience. We also believe, as we pointed out in our future predictions, that Best Buy could one day also become an enclosed "mini-mall."

For now, however, the technology companies still retain enormous power in this innovation-driven category and therefore the traditional model of distribution will likely continue for some time.

Gilt Groupe

Launched in 2007 before the economic downturn, Gilt Groupe offers flash sales of designer merchandise for men and women every day on its website, essentially making designer "sample sales" available on the web. Alexis Maybank, the company's founder, aspired to give women online access to deeply discounted designer clothes and accessories. Within two years, the site has expanded to offer merchandise for men, children and home décor, and has grown to 1.5 million members in the United States and 250,000 members in Japan, sweeping in $400 million in sales in its 2010 fiscal year, and expecting up to 25 percent growth in sales for 2011.[7]

Its business model provides one of the quintessential examples of neurological connectivity. The treasure-hunt feel of Gilt Groupe begins with its "invitation-only" membership. Once invited into this exclusive group, members feel as if they already have access to coveted pieces of apparel that most other people do not have.

Alexis Maybank explains what she has learned about the way her members shop: "It's amazing to see, because of the scarcity and time sensitivity behind our sales, the competition that goes into shopping and how commonly we hear, 'I won an item.' It's a sense of achievement, especially with the guys. It almost sounds like they're playing poker sometimes. So that's really interesting to me. We didn't expect that when we started."[8]

Shoppers rush to the site daily, then, in order not to miss something that might be gone tomorrow, they buy what they like on the spot, so that they don't lose to their "competitors" (other members). Products are usually up to 70 percent off retail prices, and include luxury fashion brands such as Derek Lam, Fendi, Calvin Klein, Herve Leger and David Yurman.

Members are sent information about upcoming sales via email. This helps to build anticipation for the shoppers, who flock to the site once the sales commence, receiving the rapid "high" in their treasure-hunt experience. This experience is about speed and timing—shoppers are allowed ten minutes to reserve items in their shopping cart during which they must decide if they want to check out. If they wait too late to browse the sale and make a purchase, "maybe someone else will have gotten to it before you," as Alexis Maybank said.[9] Simply put, their members are racing one another to get to the site first.

With the "buy now, wear now" mentality in mind, Gilt Groupe directly purchases items from the designers' current collections, getting them to shoppers quickly before the season changes and new fashion trends emerge.

Additionally, Gilt Groupe has started to create a sense of community for its members, hosting invite-only events for their members. One such example was a private early showing in the Phoenix area for the romantic comedy *When in Rome*.

What sets Gilt apart from other online sample-sale sites that have copied the model is its unparalleled, broad selection of brands. Through close-knit relationships with partners, it is able to negotiate the most popular and most recent inventory that may still be selling in department stores.

The site began with clothing, but has since expanded its merchandise offering to home, children's, and travel, reaching more consumer segments. To draw its younger audience, Gilt Groupe has launched Gilt Fuse, with more everyday casual apparel. Gilt MAN was launched to create a distinctively male shopping experience. In 2009, Gilt Groupe expanded its model and launched a new website focused on luxury vacation and travel deals, jetsetter.com. It also appears to be experimenting with fixed-price items.

At the foundation of the company are strong collaborative relationships with designers and partners, but with Gilt clearly in control of its connection with members. In fact, many designers and brands already provide proprietary products for Gilt.

Home Shopping Network

In our conversations with Home Shopping Network CEO Mindy Grossman, along with our research about HSN, we believe this business model and the way in which Grossman has transformed it from its original structure provide a powerful example supporting our thesis.

As stated on its website, HSN, Inc., is a $2.8 billion interactive multichannel retailer with strong direct-to-consumer expertise among its two operating segments, HSN and Cornerstone Brands. HSN offers innovative, differentiated retail experiences on TV, online, in catalogs, and in brick-and-mortar stores. It ships 50 million products and handles 50 million inbound customer calls annually. HSN, which created the television retail industry in 1982, now reaches 90 million homes (24 hours a day, 7 days a week, 365 days a year). HSN.com ranks in the top thirty of the top five hundred Internet retailers, is one of the top-ten trafficked e-commerce sites, and has more than a quarter million unique users every day.[10] In addition to its existing media platforms, HSN is the industry leader in technological innovation, including services such as Shop by Remote, the only service of its kind in the United States, and Video on Demand. Cornerstone Brands comprises leading home and apparel lifestyle brands like Ballard Design, Frontgate, Garnet Hill, Grandin Road, Improvements, Smith+Noble, The Territory Ahead and TravelSmith. Cornerstone Brands distributes 324 million catalogs annually, operates eight separate e-commerce sites, and runs twenty-five retail stores.

A macroview of HSN's transformation from its beginnings could be described as a transformation from a TV show that sold "stuff" to couch potatoes into a brand inviting modern consumers into Twiggy's living room in London for tea and a fun shopping experience.

From Mindy Grossman's mantra and philosophy about the brand standing for an entertaining, fun, and an exciting shopping experience that can be accessed anytime and anywhere the consumer wishes to be engaged, we heard our words: "neurological connection."

And on preemptive distribution, nobody states it more strongly: Grossman declares, "The days of trying to get a consumer to come to you are over. You really have to be in the consumer's world, wherever, whenever and however."[11]

More significantly, the way in which HSN has combined its preemptive distribution strategy with the experiences the brand promises to preemptively distribute creates a powerful synergy. In fact, the synergy of the two creates a strong neurological connection with the consumer. Indeed, the distribution platforms and the neuroexperiences become "one."

The neurological experience and the high consumers get when thinking of HSN come from their anticipation of the new and exclusive merchandise and experience that HSN promises them every day. This neurological rush is essentially a preemptive distributor for HSN because the consumer can't wait to get to the brand ahead of its competitors.

By definition, HSN distributes on all major platforms: TV; Internet; catalogs; brick-and-mortar stores; they even have over fifteen thousand videos selling products via themes on its YouTube channel, and its Facebook members are growing fast. Currently, 30 percent of revenues come from HSN.com, indicating preemption into a younger market. All these platforms, moreover, are highly integrated to achieve maximum cross-shopping benefits.

The company also introduced HSN shopping applications from mobile devices like Apple's iPhone and iTouch. CEO Grossman said of the initiative: "This new application is resonating with our customers and based on their feedback by the end of this month, we will introduce a new checkout feature in the app as well as the new interactive program guide. Leveraging this platform makes us the first retailer to stream live on three screens, TV, the Internet and mobile."[12]

The brand also seeks new distribution models. Grossman announced in 2009 at an industry conference that "we continue to take shopping to new heights having just launched the first live in-flight shopping service. Once again, we're giving the customers access to signature entertainment, lifestyle content and commerce whenever, wherever and however they choose." She continued: "Today we're still pioneering in areas of transactional innovation like Shop by Remote, the only service of its kind in the US. The distribution for this HSN interactive shopping service continues to grow with the new launch to more than 7 million Comcast subscribers and millions more to be rolled out in the coming year."[13]

HSN is also distributing the brand's image, elevating its fashion presence by forming editorial partnerships with *Elle* and *Lucky* magazines.

Further strengthening all three operating principles, HSN does not merely buy brands. They "partner with visionaries, experts and design authorities to build proprietary brands and bring them to life in unique and compelling ways. Examples include fashion authorities like Stephanie Greenfield with her successful Curations line and Eva Jeanbart-Lorenzotti of VIVRE, who had a sellout launch of her V by Eva collection during HSN's fall fashion series presented by *Elle* magazine," said CEO Grossman.[14] And it has many other proprietary and exclusive brand developments in home cooking, footwear, "fast fashion" and crafts, along with partnerships with designers such as Mark Badgley and James Mischka and celebrities like Serena Williams. HSN even innovates the creation of its own brands, such as Firm-A-Face, a technologically advanced product from one of its largest proprietary beauty brands, Serious Skin Care.

Finally, the actual experience, either on TV or online, is entertaining, educational and fun. It often use celebrities such as chef Wolfgang Puck or fashion maven Stephanie Greenfield to invite consumers into conversations, fashion shows and cooking lessons. The show's sets and themes are constantly evolving and can change in real time. For instance, if a cooking show was planned for a specific time, given updated information about what consumers are buying, HSN may change the lineup even within a given day. Hence, another dopamine rush, compelling the consumers to check in throughout the day, lest they miss something exciting.

HSN has total control of its value chain, from creation of their value—an educational, entertaining shopping experience—all the way through consumption. Its brand value also promises a broad array of merchandise available across its comprehensive preemptive distribution platforms, proprietary and/or exclusive brands; designer and celebrity brands; and much more. HSN controls the selection of the merchandise and collaborates with its vendors on presenting its brands according to the brand's positioning.

Amazon

As we've pointed out, success in the digital world requires the same application of the new rules of retailing as all other retail segments do. We have highlighted many aspects of the Amazon strategy throughout the book and explained how they fit within our framework, but we feel it necessary to explicitly highlight how Amazon adopted and embodies our principles. Indeed, as it continues to expand, we believe it is fair to speculate that Amazon is arguably now Wal-Mart's number-one competitor.

Amazon has built its brand and unique position based on its enormous array of merchandise; a highly responsive community of users who interact in many ways, including contributing reviews; and exceptional promises around fulfillment. These powerful competitive advantages have helped Amazon establish a culture of convenience and trust with its customers.

With more product categories as well as more brands and styles carried per category than its competitors, Amazon's convenience has become top-of-mind for cybershoppers thinking of making a purchase, a preemptor unto itself. The site's one-click buying strategy and superior service create an experience that is often more enjoyable, convenient and time efficient for consumers than shopping at an understaffed mall, where the ability to find what they are looking for is always in question. The customer-rating feature, even if not used, fosters the perception among vendors and customers alike that Amazon can be trusted and plays fair. Recently, a survey by Piper's Munster showed that 81 percent of Amazon's customers are satisfied with the retailer.[15] In fact, 94 percent of respondents said they would recommend Amazon to a friend. All of this has forged a deep consumer connection and has made the site the number-one destination for e-commerce.

As these points show, the strength of Amazon's competitive advantages is based on the interplay of our three principles. By controlling the value-chain, and by using innovative preemptive distribution strategies, Amazon has clearly established a deep neurological connection with consumers.

For example, neurological connectivity has been established by its tight control and superior management of returns and shipping speed and costs. Amazon is thus able to guarantee fast delivery at prices far lower than existing industry standards. For many items, shipping is free if the total order is over $25. This alone has hooked the consumer. Its Amazon Prime program invites shoppers to become members for a flat rate of $80 a year, which among other perks promises free two-day shipping. This has increased traffic and revenues across the website, and has also monetized a core group of regular customers and gained more international business. Rob

Eldridge, vice president of Amazon.com Inc., says that "across the geographies, Prime members tend to come to the site more often, shop with us more frequently, and also explore more of the different stores, so you tend to see more cross shopping."[16] And the free shipping message spreads by word of mouth from Prime users. Even for those consumers who do not purchase Prime, the knowledge of cheap or free shipping has proven irresistible.

The cost to Amazon to deliver this innovative shipping strategy, including the necessary infrastructure, was immense. Amazon estimates that the annual cost of its shipping programs in 2009 alone was $850 million.[17] The company has fulfilled this program by investing in all facets of its core operations, including its largest investment in the development of its internal network to support the operational expansion of its delivery initiatives. Specifically, to offer cheap (or free) and highly reliable shipping, Amazon built its fulfillment centers closer to its customers and logistical partners than its competitors do. For example, while most retailers distribute from a relatively small network of distribution centers to hundreds of stores, Amazon logs orders and determines shipments from multiple computerized warehouses, where products are then optimally routed via nearby UPS facilities directly to millions of customers' houses. This co-location of distribution centers with UPS hubs provides faster and less costly shipping, benefiting both Amazon and its customers. Where possible, Amazon has leveraged its technological capabilities to automate processes within warehouses and in turn minimize labor and packaging costs. This strategy in many ways is breaking the traditional tradeoff between time and price for delivery. Next in Amazon's playbook will be the same low-cost, rapid delivery for all orders! When people talk about the reason for shopping at Amazon, it is this post-transaction support that clearly makes a difference and that is almost impossible for competitors to replicate.

Amazon has also demonstrated preemptive distribution. It has been bold in coming up with new ways to get products in front of customers ahead of its competitors, either by introducing new products and services or acquiring niche websites.

With the release of the Amazon Kindle ebook reader, the company popularized the digital-reading device and essentially changed the game in the publishing and book-retail industry. It also furthered Amazon's role in the consumer-electronics industry, allowing people to carry their digital libraries in one device and limiting their selection on Amazon's gargantuan bookstore. The latest version, released in the summer of 2010, received coverage from Oprah Winfrey, boosting its sales and increasing the amount of traffic to Amazon. The Kindle has transformed the ebook industry, and with an available application for Apple's iPad and iPhone and the ability to interact with the textbook market for schools and colleges, it will only have greater power in the years ahead.

To reach a deeper segment of online shoppers—specifically, shoe and handbag buyers—Amazon made two significant moves. In 2007, the company opened Endless.com, a retail website solely offering shoes and handbags, relevant for more discrete shoppers. Then, however, it made the larger move to aquire Zappos.com in 2009, the largest acquisition in Amazon's history. Mirroring Amazon's "customer-obsessed" values, as described by its CEO, Jeffrey Bezos, Zappos has an equally powerful brand among people in the market for shoes. In comparison to the 770,000 visitors to Endless.com in June 2009, a comScore rating revealed that Zappos received 4.5 million visitors for the same month, an enormous advantage and indicative of the numbers of new customers Amazon would now have access to.

On another front, as stated in earlier chapters, we believe that the breadth and depth of Amazon's database will eventually act as a strong enabler for it to open retail stores. We envision futuristic stores that reinforce the experience users have when shopping online and that have low or nonexistent inventory, but which are really cool—maybe showcasing highest selling items around the world with terminals to order from. Perhaps customers will be able to pick up items ordered on Amazon's site.

Another preemptive potential for Amazon would be to expand into new areas that connect with its consumers on an almost daily basis. For example, with their logistics capability they are already experimenting with home delivery of online groceries, and why not?[18]

Lastly, Amazon has invested in value chain control to achieve all of this.

For example, let's examine Amazon's ten-year, $2 billion investment in developing its cloud computing initiative. A host of web services, including Amazon Simple Databases, Amazon Elastic Compute Cloud and Amazon Simple Storage are targeted toward small- and medium-sized companies who may benefit most from Amazon's leveraged web-information capabilities. Using its already developed infrastructure, Amazon is able to fulfill third-party products without incurring significant operating costs. This program has evolved into the Fulfillment by Amazon business, which Amazon uses to help increase its own shipping volume and expand its presence in the online-retail sector. One of the most important areas Amazon has excelled in is the company's control of its value chain, from the sourcing of all products sold on its site, to the warehousing and distribution of its products, to the timely, efficient and guaranteed delivery of the products and service its customers expect.

This superior managed and controlled value chain, its enormous complex of detail and technology, and equally complex operations to implement and deliver on their promises, makes Amazon an über-master across all of e-commerce.

Zappos.com

Delivering Happiness, the aptly titled new book by Tony Hsieh, CEO of and initial venture capital investor in Zappos.com, describes both

Hsieh's mantra and the heart and soul of the Zappos mission. That Zappos happens to sell shoes, apparel, handbags, accessories and beauty and household products is simply a by-product of its core business, which is to make the consumer happy. This commitment is reflected in a statement by Hsieh about the type of people he employs: "We want people who are passionate about what Zappos is about—service. I don't care if they're passionate about shoes."[19]

Delivering happiness to consumers through great customer service, then, is the basis of both Zappos' addictive neurological experience and its preemptive distribution strategy. And Zappos achieves these things by controlling the most important part of the value chain—that which connects with the consumer.

Founded in 1999 by Nick Swinmurn, Zappos was generating annual sales of a billion dollars by 2008. And with close to two thousand employees, its meteoric growth can be attributed to strategies that would appear counterintuitive to most successful businesses—but no more so than Hsieh's focus on the consumer first and profitability second.

The first stumbling block for most VCs who considered investing in Zappos was the common wisdom that no one would buy shoes without trying them on. However, Swinmurn determined that most consumers shop for specific brands of shoes. Furthermore, finding the right brand, size, style and color of shoes in traditional retail stores was a frustrating experience for shoppers. His alternative strategy was to provide an unlimited selection of shoes online. And because search-engine marketing was just beginning to emerge, he believed the Zappos model could work by identifying and attracting customers to the site and building repeat business through superior customer service.

Hsieh, a venture capitalist at the time, believed in the concept and invested several million dollars over the years, finally becoming CEO. (Hsieh had made his money in the 1998 sale of his Internet business, LinkExchange, to Microsoft for $265 million.)

Initially the business model relied on shoe brands, many of which were reluctant to partner with an online upstart, fearing erosion of their image. This, along with the fact that they were acting only as order takers, sending everything to the brands' warehouses for fulfillment, led to a repositioning decision in 2003. Hsieh determined that it was not sustainable for 25 percent of Zappos' revenues to be "drop-shipped" from warehouses not controlled by them. Counter to the commonly held belief that not owning inventory is an advantage because it mitigates risk, Hsieh was quoted in a *BusinessWeek* article as saying, "We couldn't distinguish ourselves in the eyes of our customers if we weren't going to control the entire experience . . . and we couldn't control the customer experience when a quarter of the inventory was out of our control."[20]

Declaring that "we had to give up the easy money, manage the inventory, and take the risk," Hsieh decided to reposition the brand to stand for something more than shoes. His vision was to build the model around customer service, leaving Zappos free to sell virtually any type of product.

Stellar customer service became Hsieh's big "investment," as he called it, along with owning inventory and mastering the newly emerging technology of SEM (search-engine marketing), which is less costly than traditional marketing and yields faster growth in sectors with high brand loyalty—like shoes. Today Zappos carries over four hundred shoe brands, and a thousand other brands across the other product categories mentioned above, many of them difficult to find in mainstream shopping malls.

The foundation for the "delivery of happiness" experience was the original Zappos culture, which had to come first. Without Hsieh's mantra embedded in the entire culture, its implementation would have been impossible. Early on, then, Hsieh established the now-famous "ten core values" that would define the "Zappos family culture," and ultimately drive the growth of the business. They are:

1. Deliver WOW through service (something beyond expectations, that emotionally connects and is unrelated to discounts or promotions)
2. Embrace and drive change (and most change should come from the bottom up, from those closest to the customers)
3. Create fun and a little weirdness (each individual's humor and personality should enhance the experience, making it more personal and fun)
4. Be adventurous, creative and open-minded (however risky, pursue and try new things; and make mistakes to learn from)
5. Pursue growth and learning
6. Build open and honest relationships through communication
7. Build a positive team and family spirit
8. Do more with less
9. Be passionate and determined
10. Be humble[21]

Here are a few examples of WOW experiences that have become uniquely associated with the brand and largely responsible for their success—while flying in the face of classic business strategies:

- While many companies reward sales associates on how fast they "close" the sale, particularly those using "call in" sales from the Internet and catalogs, Zappos urges its associates to spend as much time as necessary to build a relationship and create a WOW experience. And it scores all calls on the basis of how helpful its associates were. Accordingly, its customer service center is open 24/7, and each new employee goes through four weeks of training.
- Zappos photographs each newly received shoe style from eight different angles for the customer's ease of selection.
- All shipping is free, and Zappos strives for next-day delivery.

- To offset concerns about buying shoes with the wrong fit, Zappos has a free return shipping policy, good for one year following purchase.
- If Zappos runs out of a given item, or it doesn't carry a brand requested, the sales reps are encouraged to provide the caller with other online sites, including competitors.

For these and many other reasons, Zappos represents one of the true masters in all of retailing, delivering a unique neurological experience, which by itself preempts competitors and has made it the go-to site for consumers. And it has achieved this preeminence by taking control of its value chain early on.

So the meteoric rise of Zappos is clearly attributable to the three operating principles of our thesis, which also led to their acquisition by Amazon.com in November 2009. When that happened, Tony Hsieh delivered an open letter to his employees, stating "We learned that they (Amazon) truly wanted us to continue in our own unique way. I think 'unique' was their way of saying 'fun and a little weird.'"[22]

Apple

We could not end this chapter without tipping our hat to perhaps the true Master: Apple.

With so much having been said about this company, there is no need to repeat its history or the story of its growth, but there is one aspect we would like to highlight, and that is the decision that Apple made to open stores. As we have predicted, we believe that Amazon, eBay and other pure e-commerce sites will open stores, and that retailers will one day create branded mini-malls within their four walls. And every successful retailer or consumer-facing company will accelerate its investments in creating a great in-store experience.

Apple's decision to open stores was a brilliant strategy, in which it's providing an unequalled neurological experience and gaining preemptive distribution. (And, of course, it totally controls its value chain.) Microsoft is now playing catch-up. The question is whether it can execute to the Apple standard.

Apple realized that it could control, shape and determine the emotional connection that customers have with Apple by opening stores. In doing so every channel of distribution—online sales, sales through Best Buy, etc.—would be enhanced and the connection with the consumer would be intensified. Starting with their anticipation of a fun shopping experience, when they get to the Apple store, their first step is into the "box," branded with the iconic Apple logo. It is the beginning of what CEO Steve Jobs calls the "Apple user experience." Apple stores have a distinctive futuristic interior and interactive, pristine display tables. All stores share glass and anodized aluminum paneling.

Once inside, friendly, enthusiastic and technologically sophisticated sales reps engage and put the customers at ease while they introduce them to products and explain any of the attributes the consumer needs help with. The white interior with splashes of the color wheel evokes the user-friendly, yet vibrant experience of owning a Mac product. The experience is never dull.

Even though all the stores are relatively new, they are constantly being improved. Peter Oppenheimer, Apple's CFO, remarks: "We are seeing strong results from our remodeled stores. [We have remodeled] seventy-two of the stores to bring them to our most updated design. And those designs are providing the best customer experience in the industry bar none, whether it be up front in the selling part of the store or certainly in the back of the store, with the Genius Bars or the creative bars. And customers are having a great experience."[23]

The Genius Bar supports the advertised user-friendly factor. Serving as Apple's tech support and repairs team within every store, it is so popular that customers must make an appointment or wait at least an hour, sometimes two. However, the so-called geniuses are exclusively trained at troubleshooting products and helping people with their technological questions.

Like the retail stores, the simplicity and style in product offerings and physicality are competitive advantages of Apple's brand. We don't want to downplay the genius of the product development at the heart of the company. That feature is obvious. When the iPod / iTunes launched, it was a game changer in the consumer electronics and digital music industry. The push forward into physical stores, however, was not obvious even with that product success. Only if you believe that you need to control the consumer experience to achieve extraordinary success would you have made this move. We believe that the data are proving this to be true in every consumer business.

And of course control of the value chain has also been crucial to Apple's success. For example, Apple's five-year exclusive partnership with AT&T gave Apple unprecedented control over the development and branding of the iPhone. Value-chain control extends to maintaining tight licensing structures around all Apple's products.

On all three principles we see Apple as the true Master.

CHAPTER 11

THE TURNAROUND ARTISTS

MASTERS RETURNING?

Not only did the iconic "merchant Prince," CEO Millard ("Mickey") Drexler, revive the core Gap brand in the early 1980s, but he also launched Old Navy, repositioned Banana Republic and gave all three brands clear and distinct positions for three equally defined consumer segments. Indeed, all three were energetic, dominant and fast-growing businesses throughout the 1990s. They were not only relevant and enormously desired by each of their well-defined consumer groups, they had also achieved a neurological connection. Consumers could not seem to get enough of the brands, particularly the Gap. The Gap brand was, it seemed, the simplest definition of "cool."

To feed and capitalize on this enormous demand, the Gap aggressively pursued a preemptive distribution strategy, opening a total of about three thousand stores in the United States and Canada by the end of the decade. It also extended the brand by launching Gap Kids, Gap Body, Gap Maternity and Baby Gap, with all these lines available online as well. The Gap grew to annual revenues of about $15 billion, making it the largest apparel retailer in the United States at the time.

Then several things happened. Not all at once, but concurrently enough to tip the ship. Despite a relentless stream of competitive entrants into the Gap's space during the 1990s, it seemed as though the Gap couldn't open stores fast enough. Wall Street and its shareholders were both demanding this rapid growth. This is the same pressure that has driven many public companies to make short-term tactical decisions for quarterly results, while strategic decisions to sustain competitive advantage over the long term are postponed.

As a result of this rapid growth, Drexler admitted to a Goldman Sachs annual conference, he was distracted from his typical role of keeping consumers' pulse. Too many layers of management took him too far away from those areas of the business that touched the consumer: product, presentation, communications, advertising, service, environment and image. In short, he lost control over the experience, including the neurological connection.

Additionally, as competitors began to ape the casual fashion that was its signature, Gap redirected its merchandising strategy toward trendier looks, edging away from its core competency. Trendy, alas, does not always equal cool.

So two major problems were beginning to emerge, both equally deleterious to the brand's powerful connection with consumers. First, the poorly planned rapid growth turned preemptive distribution into *ubiquitous* distribution, occupying retail space wherever it could be found. Ubiquity is the antithesis of cool to the Gap's core consumers—the young. And the second problem was the Gap's expanding merchandise lines for its various brand extensions, thus blurring what the original core brand stood for.

Accompanying the growth was a growing bureaucracy, which took Drexler away from what he does best. He lost focus on the product, the brand's soul, the environment, and, as mentioned, the all-important shopping experience. As a result, the Gap lost its neurological consumer connection.

And while Drexler was caught in the Gap's growth maelstrom, he was helpless to prevent the simultaneous declines of Banana Republic and Old Navy. Old Navy lost its consumer connection as "cheap chic" and Banana Republic went from work attire to expensive dressy.

As it all started to come apart at the end of the 1990s, the Gap experienced two years of declining sales, and Drexler began to close stores and cut costs as he struggled to right the brand and reconnect with consumers. He departed in 2002.

Is This Master Returning?

Following some initial rays of hope for Drexler's successor, Paul Pressler from Disney Stores, the rush to failure resumed, and between June 2004 and December 2006 (eight months before Pressler would be replaced), comparative store sales declined in every month but three (those stores opened for more than a year as a measure of real growth based on consumer demand as opposed to the opening of a new store which simply gets new traffic).

Glenn Murphy, previously CEO of a Canadian drug store chain, joined Gap Stores as CEO in July 2007. By the middle of 2008, the Gap was still struggling, with same-store sales continuing to decline. In fact, sales were the same as they were three years prior to his arrival, at around $15 billion.

And remember that even while struggling to repair the brands, the enterprise still must face the day-to-day challenges inherent in all retail businesses.

Although the Gap has control (buyer power) over its suppliers (it actively monitors sewing and other production functions), it must continually find lower-cost manufacturers to stay competitive. The Gap has over seven hundred suppliers, who are continually monitored for acceptable working conditions, which gets reported in the Gap's Social Responsibility Report.

Also, amid the turmoil of two CEO changes in five years, the Gap lost key design talent. And while repositioning a brand involves many elements, design is right at the top. Given that the recapturing of "cool" requires a quick response to trends, it's hard to see how a giant, floundering enterprise can get it back.

Can the Master Return?

There are many reasons to be optimistic in response to this question. For example, the capability still exists at the Gap of re-creating a neuroconnection so that consumers will once again want to embrace the brand for how it makes them feel.

The Gap's recent resuscitation of the denim brand with the "cool" recycling program of "1969 Denim" clearly worked for the consumer. Also, its newfound focus on social responsibility and environmental awareness appeal to its young and progressive clientele. As reported in a May 3, 2010 article in the *Epoch Times,* the Gap won the 2010 Social Innovation Award.[1] Around one hundred firms were part of this two-year program, and there were eleven winners who had developed innovative programs that focus on social responsibility (think: "self to community"). The Gap won the award for its GAP Inc. P.A.C.E. (Personal Advancement, Career Enhancement) program for women garment workers. P.A.C.E. was formed in India in 2007 and helps female textile industry employees move up the career ladder through education and training provided by the company. For the fourth year, the Gap received the World's Most Ethical Company award in the specialty retail sector.

The control of the value chain enables the Gap to work with new designers, and reduces cycle times so that it can deliver more "cool" new merchandise on a rapid, more frequent basis. The key metric for the improvement at the Gap will be shrinking decision-making times, essentially implementing a "speed-to-market" strategy. Historically this has been a major problem for the company. Its enormous infrastructure, accompanied by layers of management, has continuously caused frustration about the pace of getting things done.

The opportunity for the Gap to streamline internally, speed up all its processes and to deliver more "cool" products and experiences is immense. And so far, the company appears to be taking advantage of this. Consumers are returning to the store more often to check out the "new and now" products.

There is, however, a substantial Wave III challenge facing the company. As consumers seek more "special for me" brands, as opposed to mega-brands, the Gap is inevitably still a mega-brand.

We believe the Gap must address this immutable consumer shift. It will likely find its brand defined as too large and overexposed. But if it is to succeed, it must develop a precisely targeted preemptive distribution strategy, and, more important, it must reconnect neurologically with consumers.

Starbucks

How Howard Schultz Talked the Starbucks Talk,
then Walked the Wall Street Walk

When Starbucks' chairman, Howard Schultz, bought Starbucks in 1987, his vision was that it would become the "third place" between work and home. This vision alone turns most retailers' view of their businesses on its head. His original mission statement—"We're not in the coffee business, serving people. We're in the people business, serving coffee"—was made some time ago, but it's certainly timeless. How many retailers think this way about their businesses? And even if there are a few, how many actually run their businesses by putting people before product? And what does it mean to do that?

It means that it's not about what the retailer is selling; it's about what it does to that space (building, website, etc.) that makes the consumer want to buy. It's about turning the space into such a compelling experience that consumers want to seek it out. And once they enter that brand, you must envelop them in a total neurological experience. Then they will buy more than ever before. Just ask Starbucks if consumers will pay more than an item appears to be worth for that experience. Everyone knows what the answer is.

We believe Starbucks was the quintessential, perhaps even the first, example of a neurologically connective brand. Schultz and his "family" of employees did, in fact, create a third place. First of all, they hired baristas and other young people based primarily on their social skills. The experience—from the evocation of an inviting living room, to the sound of coffee grinding and the smell of it freshly roasting, to the chatty interaction between "family" and guests—touched all five human senses, and the all-important sixth sense: the mind. Indeed, it was a place where people could hang out, read the paper, make friends and generally wrap themselves in the romance of an Italian-style espresso bar.

Starbucks won and owned so much of the coffee share of consumers' minds that "Starbuckians," at the mere thought of the brand, felt a dopamine rush and literally could not get there fast enough.

The Power of the Neuroconnection and Preemptive Distribution

While Schultz may not have explicitly described the experience as neurologically connecting with his consumers, he also would not have described the fact that he wanted to rapidly share the experience with the entire world as preemptive distribution. And he probably would not have acknowledged that the only reason he could implement both, and thus achieve his goals, was because he had total control over his value chain (in fact, Starbucks even controlled the bean farms).

Nevertheless, new CEO Jim Donald's mantra was "I want to grow big and stay small at the same time. We want to run the company just like we did when we were one store on Pike Place Market in Seattle."[2]

And grow big and grow globally it did.

In 1992 Starbucks went public, and between 1995 and 2005 alone it grew from under a thousand stores to over ten thousand. In that period, its comparable store sales growth never went below 5 percent, and averaged around 7 percent. Its stock price soared during the period by 5000 percent.

The "Wall Street Walk" Begins

In 2005, Starbucks was not shy about its long-term goal, to reach twenty-five to thirty thousand stores, up from its ten thousand at

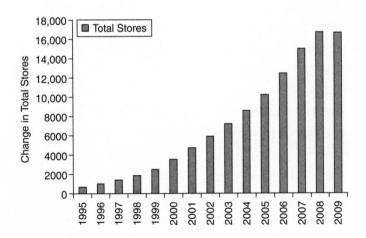

Figure 11.1: Total stores

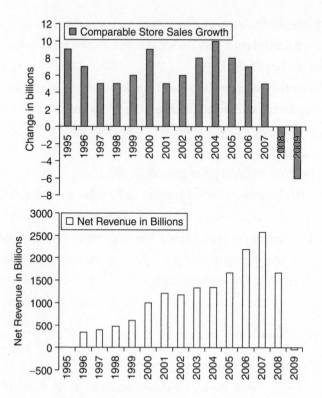

Figure 11.2: Comparable store sales growth

the time. Between 2005 and 2009 it almost doubled its number of locations, reaching 16,680. And, at the time, it was projecting top-line growth of 20 percent and bottom-line of 23–25 percent over the next three to five years.

Think of those stores as thirty thousand human fingers reaching out to touch customers with the neurological experience they desire and expect. And where are all those experiential shops going to be?

The Warriors of Preemptive Distribution

Making the neuroconnection so compelling that consumers would seek it out was one thing. But the Starbucks team of "share warriors" also understood the principle of preemptive access/distribution, of extending its human touch as close to its consumers as possible, making the Starbucks dream more accessible.

It planned to get to smaller cities, and expand globally to Europe and the Far East, including China and India. Indeed, Starbucks was in the business of satisfying consumers' dreams first—coffee just happened to be one part of the dream.

But then several things happened on the way to its dream of spreading around the world.

From Preemption to Ubiquity

In 2007, an internal memo written by Howard Schultz, criticizing the loss of some of the "romance and theater" along its growth trajectory, was leaked to the press. At the time, it raised the question of whether Schultz intended to act on his feelings.

The memo, sent to then-CEO Jim Donald on February 14, 2007, was self-chastising in that it questioned the effects of specific changes to the Starbucks experience that he himself had authorized along the way. At various points along its meteoric rise, operating efficiencies and productivity improvements were employed to abet and accelerate the growth.

For example, the installation of automatic espresso machines "solved a major problem in terms of speed of service and efficiency. . . . At the same time, we overlooked the fact that we would remove much of the romance and theater" (Starbucks baristas used to pull espresso shots by hand). Furthermore, he added, "that became even more damaging . . . as the machines blocked the visual sightline the customer previously had to watch the drink being made, and for the intimate experience with the barista."

Starbucks also switched to "flavor locked packaging," which eliminated the scooping of fresh beans out of bins and grinding it in front of customers. Schultz observed, "We achieved fresh roasted bagged coffee, but at what cost? The loss of aroma—perhaps the most powerful non-verbal signal we had in our stores. In fact, I am not sure people today even know we are roasting coffee. You certainly can't get the message from being in our stores."

The store designs were also standardized, and according to Schultz it created "stores that no longer have the soul of the past. . . . Some people even call our stores sterile, cookie cutter."

Another comparable-store growth strategy was the addition of other product offerings: food (which Schultz originally said he would never add), books and music. It also added a drive-through capability. Ironically, the fast-food and drive-through features began to position them in the competitive sphere of McDonald's and Dunkin' Donuts, both of whom were trying to emulate Starbucks coffee, if not its whole experience. In fact, some research at the time found higher customer loyalty among Dunkin's customers than those of Starbucks.

Schultz's assessment of the decisions he made in favor of growth was stated in the memo: "Over the past ten years, in order to achieve growth, development, and scale necessary to go from less than 1,000 stores to 13,000 and beyond, we have had to make a series of decisions that, in retrospect, have led to the watering down of the Starbucks experience and what some might call the commoditization of our brand. Many of these decisions were probably right at the time, and on their own merit would not have created the dilution of experience; but in this case, the sum is much greater and, unfortunately, much more damaging than the individual pieces."[3]

Is This Master Returning?

Howard Schultz did return as CEO in 2008 to return the "master" brand that he had created back to its number-one position as a "third place" neurological experience.

Is he getting the job done?

In February 2008, Starbucks captured the attention of the business world when it boldly closed 7,100 of its stores for three hours so that it could retrain its baristas on creating a Starbucks-branded customer service experience, essentially returning to its original experiential roots.

In March 2008, Schultz announced a new espresso system and said that pre-ground beans would no longer be used. "We are returning to the very best elements of our heritage and bringing back the simple romance and excitement of coffee," said Schultz.[4] "Since 1971, we have sourced, roasted and sold the world's finest coffees. By highlighting that history through Pike Place Roast, and bringing back the sounds and aromas of the coffeehouse, we are raising the bar on what it means to serve the perfect cup of coffee."[5] That year, according to an April 2, 2009 *Retailer Daily* article, Starbucks closed 900 stores, eliminated 6700 jobs and announced a 69 percent drop in profits during one quarter.[6] Customers started "Save our Starbucks" petitions and websites. And all customers were encouraged to get involved in the process of improving Starbucks by posting ideas to the My Starbucks website.

In January 2009, it announced that net income had fallen to $64.3 million, and revenue had fallen to $2.62 billion from $2.77 billion, while analysts had predicted revenue of $2.70 billion that month. Following that drop, in February 2009 Starbucks announced that another 616 stores would be closed.[7]

In February 2010 some industry blogs reported that Starbucks was looking into offering "pour over" brew method coffee. This would be like the Blue Bottle method of brewing single-drip coffee.

Moreover, as its weakening brand and ubiquity were further hammered by the Great Recession, Starbucks' competition did not sleep. It is facing challenges from traditional fast-food and bakery chains such as McDonald's, Dunkin' Donuts and Panera Bread, which are selling specialty coffee drinks at reduced prices. Starbucks also competes with local premium-priced cafes that now offer the "third place" experience. As stated in a blog post by Sarah Gilbert, "Starbucks is being squeezed into an uncomfortable middle ground between the low-price, blue collar product on one end (Dunkin' Donuts) and the eco-friendly, high-quality product on the other end (Juan Valdez). The only thing it has going to keep its profits from splattering all over the wall is customer loyalty . . . and oatmeal. Will it survive?"[8]

Schultz is between a rock and a hard place, but he did not lose his customers overnight, and he will not recover them overnight, if at all. The major question is, assuming he reinstates an even better neurological experience, will those customers he wants to recover give him the time to do so, when there are now so many equally compelling choices elsewhere? One thing is clear—the entire strategy hinges on the ability to create a true "experience" for the consumer inside the store. If Via, its new instant coffee brand, is going to have sustained resonance in the supermarkets, it will be because people associate it with the Starbucks experience in the stores. If that experience remains strong and powerful, Schultz's wholesale strategy for growth will succeed.

We believe Schultz understands this. He's certainly investing in it. And our bet would follow his. His increasing sales tell us that consumers are again seeking that Zen moment with a cup of coffee, and Starbucks was the über game-changer that originally provided it. Can Schultz bring it back?

We shall see.

CHAPTER 12

LESSONS FROM SEARS

SUCCESS TO STRUGGLE

Two of the most frequently asked questions from retail executives, employees and investors during our research were:

1. Are there examples of major retailers that responded to the vast consumer and market shifts from Wave I to II, and successfully transformed their business strategies and models accordingly?
2. If a retailer fails to successfully transform its business in Wave III, according to your thesis, how difficult is it to turn the business around?

These questions are not academic. While we have provided many examples throughout the book of retailers and wholesalers that are transforming themselves in Wave III, with varying degrees of success, you always need a benchmark to measure yourself against.

Our research led us to an obvious choice for closer analysis.

Sears, Roebuck and Co., founded in 1886, embodies the successful shift from Wave I to II, making its current struggle to navigate Wave III even more instructive. Its current search for a relevant value proposition is instructive to every company wondering whether it can turn itself around.

We also chose Sears to explore these questions because, while every company has its own quirks, the Sears story also has many universal components.

As we discussed in chapters 1 and 2, Sears was arguably the most successful retailer during both Waves I and II, responding to the marketplace characteristics that drove success in both waves. Among the most notable shifts were two in particular.

From Catalogs to Stores
to the Mass Markets of Wave II

In the late 1800s, before the Internet was even imagined, the famous Sears catalog gave it the same advantage that innovative e-commerce sites have over brick-and-mortar retailers today. Essentially, Sears was distributing its entire store into the living rooms of America's middle class, whose shopping options were slim, and in many cases too impractical. As we pointed out in earlier chapters, the catalog contained everything those families would ever need, from cradle to grave, at affordable prices. And if they couldn't pay it all at once, Sears would help them out with payment terms.

Those families also could not wait to see the new catalog every month in anticipation of exciting new products. More and more of those products were exclusive to, and some even produced by, Sears. In this Sears was truly on the leading edge of vertical integration and value-chain control.

Because its different aspects were so closely intertwined, Sears grew just as rapidly as America's middle class. Then, as the population began migrating from rural areas to the newly forming towns, cities and then suburbs, and particularly after the construction of the interstate highway system, Sears adjusted its preemptive strategy to ensure that its stores were the first ones to reach consumers in their new neighborhoods. In fact, Sears was the developer and ultimate anchor for the very first shopping centers in the country, and expanded along with the mall movement across the United States.

Sears thus expanded its strategy through multidistribution platforms and physically demonstrated the extent of its investment in the consumer. Sears was beginning to become untouchable.

From Retail Marketer to Branded Mass Marketer of Lifestyle Brands

In the early 1960s, Sears' merchandising supervisor was James Button. Schooled in research psychology at the University of Chicago, he brought the concept of marketing to Sears. Known as a bit of an enigma, Button had a view of marketing that embodied all the activities of value creation, including research and development, branding/imaging, communications/advertising, publicity and distribution. These functions were arguably nonexistent in most retail businesses at the time.

Button increased the size of Sears' R & D lab, introduced a market-research department and process and advanced the company's understanding of advertising. He firmly believed that relentless consumer research and product development and testing (as opposed to gut instinct) were the only sure paths to successful innovation.

And successful they were. A constant stream of brands and products were rolled out through the largest distribution machine in the world. The number of "firsts" and private and exclusive Sears brands was mind-boggling: the first steel-belted radial tire;

Craftsman tools; DieHard batteries; Kenmore appliances; Tough-skin jeans; Cling-alon hosiery; the Comfort Shirt; the NFL and Winnie-the-Pooh exclusive licenses; and many others. These exclusive brands were made possible by Sears' unique merchandising structure and process. As the owner of many of its suppliers, or as the primary buyer from others, its vertical integration facilitated a continuous process of joint research, innovation, testing and therefore a continuous stream of new and exclusive products and brands. It provided the foundation of Sears' value proposition, and was an enormous advantage over competitors.

A vital characteristic of these relationships was the mutual reverence, loyalty and trust that bound Sears' merchandisers and suppliers. In fact, Sears would often fund suppliers' production or buy ingredient products in volume for several suppliers, reducing costs for the benefit of both. Sears also used its knowledge of suppliers' costs, along with a promise of huge-volume orders, to negotiate the lowest possible price for the goods.

Button's genius gave consumers some of the greatest products and brands the world has ever known, all exclusive to Sears. And his underlying strategy—which went largely unnoticed, even by Sears' management and consultants at the time—was to pursue product innovations for *all* consumers. His open acknowledgment of their desires for better quality and better performance, and for honest, low prices, made Sears a "democratic" retailer. It was a resource for all Americans, not just the middle class. High- and low-income consumers of all ages and genders shopped at Sears. Thus, it had a unique niche—in the sense that it wasn't niche at all. Button's approach reflected the outlook of Sears' CEO at the time, Robert Wood, who said, "The customer is your employer, and the moment we lose their confidence is the beginning of the disintegration of the company."[1]

Sears did not have to compete head-on with the department stores (because it had its own exclusive brands) or with the discounters (they couldn't operate on the higher cost structure necessary to match Sears' offerings). Most important, Sears' sales associates were the early equivalent of Best Buy's "blue shirts" or "Geek Squad." They were thoroughly trained and proficient in the Sears "rule book"; they could instruct customers how to use every brand and product in their area.

Furthermore, all Sears stores were decentralized when it came to merchandise decisions. Therefore, store managers ordered and bought the products and quantities according to their local consumers' preferences. Through this localization, there was a clear competitive advantage.

In Wave II, Sears was the equivalent of Wal-Mart today. And it powered into the 1970s as an unparalleled master of retailing, bigger than the next five largest retailers combined, with 900 large stores and over 2600 smaller retail and catalog outlets, accounting for 1 percent of the gross national product.[2] More than half the households in the country had a Sears credit card, and a survey at the time confirmed that it was the most trusted economic institution in the country.[3]

Then, in the mid to late 1970s, the unraveling began. Tragically, after eighty-four years of building one of the greatest brands the world had ever seen, it would take Sears just a few years to lose its unique competitive position and veer into a quarter century of decline that continues to this day. What happened?

Misreading the Tea Leaves

Sears conducted a major study in the early 1970s that alerted them to the following major shifts, which were exacerbated by growing market saturation and the slowing economy:

- Sears' customer base was getting older and turning into two-income families, and women were becoming the most important shoppers.

- The youth of America were not getting married as early as their parents had, and they were seeking their own shopping sources, such as the rapidly growing specialty chains.
- Sears' profitability was shifting from merchandise, which had been contributing 80–90 percent of profits, to services, which were contributing 75 percent by the end of the 1970s (including installation, credit extension and its Allstate insurance business).
- Competitors were closing the gap—JCPenney in the malls and Kmarts appearing on every corner. The specialty store upstarts were also staking a claim in the malls, and Wal-Mart was a preview of coming attractions.[4]

The result of this study, along with many other internal issues that were coming to a head, included political infighting between stores and merchandising management; mounting costs; and a calcifying culture, ultimately forcing Sears management to seek a new direction. They began to believe that the key to growth was not to be found in the core competencies that had driven the success of the company. They started to look into new businesses that would be complementary and synergistic. (Not coincidentally, this was also the period in Wave II when the trends and "drivers" that would fuel the growth of the successful retail models in Wave III began to emerge.) Sears moved in a completely different direction.

This was the critical juncture in Sears' history. Had the visionary leadership of CEO Arthur Wood and the brilliant James Button remained in place, Sears might have successfully executed the necessary strategic changes to meet the challenges and maintain its unique competitive position. This did not happen.

Wood's successor, Edward Telling, was plucked from store management (or "the field," as they called it, as opposed to the "parent," where the merchandising and marketing departments resided). The field had grown to five powerful regional organizations that operated like fiefdoms, and their infighting with merchandising and marketing grew proportionately. Telling, the most powerful of the five heads, in charge of the Northeast region, was the first CEO to be selected from the field.

With Telling in charge, it did not take long for the field heads to begin gaining in the turf wars and for the influence of James Button to be diminished. Then Button became ill and resigned toward the end of the 1970s.

Even as the Sears Tower was going up as the company's new Chicago headquarters, much of its world, inside and outside, was starting to crack. And to make matters worse, the larger economy was tanking.

While Sears' profits were plummeting in 1979 and 1980 because of the combination of inflation-raging interest rates, rising operating costs, loss of direction, mounting competition and organizational disarray, Telling determined that the retail business had matured, and retreated to the Tower with his new team to work on building what he called the "Great American Company": Sears as a diversified conglomerate of financial, real estate and insurance services. At the same time, he elevated Edward A. Brennan, another "field" man, to head up the retail business. Ironically, Brennan was charged with saving what truly *was* the Great American Company—the Sears retail business. At this crucial crossroads in Sears' history, the chief executive was leaving the scene of the disaster to chase his dreams.

That dream was of a great synergy between financial services and the core retail business. Sears already owned Allstate Insurance, and it went on to acquire Dean Witter Reynolds financial services, Coldwell Banker real estate and, later, Discover Card. It also created the Sears U.S. Government Money Market Trust Fund and formed the Sears World Trade Company. The synergy was to come from Sears using its stores, catalogs and Allstate Insurance offices as additional locations where they could insert the financial services businesses. It expected to lure the millions of Sears customers across the aisle to purchase financial services, and vice versa. Telling boasted to the press about their "socks and stocks" strategy.

Chief among the several factors necessary for this grand strategy to work, however, was a successful and growing core retail business to generate the crossover and new traffic expected. But this was not the case. Not only was the core business beginning to decline during this period, but the customers also questioned Sears' authority on financial skills and management, citing confusion about where in their lives Sears now belonged. What was it—retailer, banker, financier, real estate mogul or the "money store"? What did it stand for?

In the end, rather than an inspired synergy, Telling's so-called Great American Company was one of the first major strategy missteps that sent Sears into its long decline. In fact, the strategy likely caused a reverse downward synergy. Along with the already daunting task of turning the retail business around, Telling's idea to "bolt on" a completely different business just compounded the complexity and confusion of accomplishing either.

Carol Farmer, a retail consultant at the time declared: "If Sears executives can't run the business they know—retailing—why should we think they'll be able to do any better running a business they don't know?"[5]

So Telling's dream did not come true. In fact, the financial services businesses might as well have been independent entities of a holding company. They ended up contributing only incrementally (with the exception of Allstate, which Sears held even before Telling, and eventually the Discover Card). By the early 1990s all the financial services, real estate and insurance businesses were sold off as Sears entered another decade-long search for direction.

The 1980s: Up Again, Down Again, Part I

The new head of retail, Edward Brennan, did make some bold moves in the early 1980s, enough to achieve a short-lived spike in business and confirm his promotion to CEO in 1984 upon Telling's retirement. Some of his initiatives for a "new Sears" included: improving stores and merchandise presentations; adding national brands; trying to strengthen apparel lines; launching a "Store of the Future" concept as a template for refurbishing stores over a five-year period; rolling out Business System Centers and paint and hardware specialty stores (a beginning probe for competing in the specialty tier); and the launch of a national ad campaign.

However, all these initiatives turned out to be merely opportunistic tactics. The ad campaign's underlying message said it all: *Sears has everything.* So while Sears gained a momentary boost through Brennan's initiatives, it had definitely lost its once-supreme position and still lacked a clear strategic direction.

The once-proud culture turned arrogant, then bureaucratic. The constructive balance between stores and merchandising and marketing deteriorated into constant infighting. This conflict, along with the loss of Button's private and exclusive branding strategy (giving way to national brands) and cost cutting, led to the unraveling of Sears' fully integrated (and/or exclusively controlled) product development and production sourcing. This was further exacerbated when it shuttered its R & D and consumer research departments.

Sears' small-store strategy, also initiated under Brennan, would prove to be too little too late, as well as underfunded, since more capital was being infused into the financial services business. Finally, it was confronting the arrival of Wal-Mart as the new, hot discounter in small towns. Cutbacks in store expansion also left many of its original stores anchored in declining locations.

For ten years Sears focused on the so-called synergy for growing financial services while ignoring the store. The "store of the future" was a flop. An everyday-low-price branding strategy failed. During the 1970s and '80s total retail space doubled in the United States, while Sears concentrated on closing and remodeling. It halfheartedly dabbled in specialty store concepts that turned out to be too late and insufficiently funded.

Sears' return on equity (ROE) in 1984 was at 14 percent. In 1992 it stood at 9.6 percent. Virtually all of Sears' earnings between 1985 and 1992 came from the financial services businesses. And, for all Sears' numerous cost reduction efforts during the 1980s, its cost-to-sales ratio continued to be almost double that of Wal-Mart and well above the rest of its competitors.

Finally, with the $3 billion sale of the financial services business, which at the time was claimed to have reduced debt, many pundits said there would not be enough left for capital spending on the stores.

Sears was not only on a severely declining revenue and income trajectory; it was waffling on a strategic positioning in the no-man's-land of "everything to everybody." Therefore, it was competing against the discounters from below, the department stores from above, the specialty stores in front and the newly emerging big-box specialists. In the process, Sears had become a traditional retailer instead of the greatest brand and marketer with the strongest consumer connection the country had ever known.

It was time for a new leader.

The 1990s: Up Again, Down Again, Part II

In 1992, Arthur Martinez became only the second leader from outside Sears in its history ("General" Robert Wood being the first). By then Sears had shed all its financial services businesses.

Martinez came in with a strategic vision for Sears and developed a plan for fundamental transformation, primarily focusing on women's apparel, with an advertising slogan emphasizing "The Softer Side of Sears." Having come from the Saks department stores, he would also move Sears into more of a department-store positioning. This and other strategic initiatives showed initial success. By 1997–1998, revenues had increased about 30 percent to roughly $36 billion, and profits rose from losses of close to $3 billion to a gain of over $1 billion.

However, when sales and income started to drop in 1998, there was speculation that the seemingly spectacular turnaround may in fact have been due to Sears' aggressive focus on growing its credit card business, beginning in 1993. By 1997, 60 percent of all sales transactions were done with credit cards, and experts suggested that over 60 percent of Sears' bottom line was coming from the credit business.[6]

Despite the potential of the credit business as the growth engine for the retail business, though, Martinez simply could not change the culture of Sears. In fact, in Martinez's later book *The Hard Road to the Softer Side: Lessons from the Transformation of Sears,* he stated that toward the end of his tenure, he felt Sears was falling back into the same trap he inherited when he took over in 1992: "Just do more of the same, only work harder." He was also asking himself the same question as when he arrived: "What is this company going to be? What does it stand for?"[7]

At the end of the 1990s, then, Sears had no more of a strategic compass than it had ten years before. It was time for yet another leader.

The 2000s: Slowly Sinking During Wave III

When Alan Lacy was made CEO in 2001, he immediately moved to grab the low-hanging fruit by doing what he had done best as

CFO under Martinez. He slashed costs and further pumped up the credit business. Lacy would be the fourth nonmerchant in a row to run the company, and the second, after Martinez, with a primarily financial background.

In less than a year, the *Wall Street Journal* reported that Lacy was considering abandoning the apparel business altogether, after a 25 percent drop in net income in the first quarter of 2001. He himself admitted at an analyst meeting that Sears could not find its place in fashion, stating, "We almost don't have any personality."[8] As apparel growth slipped, critics increasingly took shots at Martinez's efforts, which now appeared short-lived. However, Lacy realized that the cost of radically changing stores and replacing lost clothing sales (stagnant, at about $8 billion) would be too steep.

By 2003, Sears had experienced eighteen consecutive months of sales declines, and the credit business was responsible for over two-thirds of total net income. In reaction, Sears bought Lands' End, thereby going deeper into the apparel category, where it had had no success since the late 1970s.

If Martinez lost his control of the culture, Lacy was losing it on all fronts. Sears still didn't know what it stood for. Indeed, Sears seemed to be poised for its final descent. Adjusted for inflation, Sears' volume declined about 20 percent from its pinnacle in the late 1970s, and continues to drop today.

The Lessons Learned So Far

We believe Sears' successful migration from Wave I into Wave II was because it evolved across three key business dimensions:

1. The shift from a production-driven model to one of marketing and demand creation (with a flow of new and exclu-

sive products and brands, and developing sophisticated marketing and advertising strategies)

2. Expanding its distribution platforms (catalogs, stores), initiating and anchoring shopping centers and malls; all following the population migration from rural areas to towns, cities and then suburbs

3. Building the infrastructure and supplier relations necessary to support this model

Interestingly, these principles are in many ways early versions of the principles we believe drive success today. And Sears' original model implemented these strategies far more effectively than its competitors, much like Wal-Mart does today.

However, as the major Wave III consumer, competitive and marketplace shifts began to occur, enabled by technology and globalization, Sears made three fundamental missteps:

1. It concluded that market saturation meant growth had to come from businesses outside its "core." This did not have to be fatal; however, it starved the resources (capital and management) from the retail business, making it unable to respond and adapt to the evolving needs of the Wave III consumer and marketplace.

2. It allowed the emergence of a bureaucratic culture, which slowed decision making. When the unraveling began in the late 1970s, Sears' culture became characterized by infighting and significant strategic redirects. This cultural sclerosis is a disease that cripples many large, older companies in need of change for survival.

3. It stopped investing in new distribution formats.

We believe these are key lessons for all retailers attempting to make a successful shift into Wave III.

Sears as It Struggles into Wave III

In 2004, a strategic financial visionary named Edward "Eddie" Lampert came to the rescue. Head of his own hedge fund, ESL Investments, and a former Goldman Sachs risk arbitrageur, Lampert has a genius for spotting great deals among distressed companies that he considers to be undervalued. He then buys a major stake at a bargain price.

Having made such a deal for the equally distressed Kmart a couple years before his move on Sears, he combined the two companies under the name Sears Holdings (to be owned by ESL Investments, with Lampert owning 41 percent of the stock.) He and his newly appointed team declared to Wall Street and the world that they were going to return Kmart and Sears to their rightful positions as successful, iconic retail brands.

In keeping with his track record, Lampert and his team slashed costs across the boards to boost per-share earnings and improve returns on capital, even though both retailers were hemorrhaging before he bought them. Comparative store sales were, and still are, declining month-over-month. However, by cutting people, advertising and research costs and slashing store maintenance and capital improvements, he improved profitability and share prices. Lampert could then leverage the earnings and cash to invest in more promising growth opportunities with higher returns—not necessarily back into the dying businesses.

After several years of cost cutting, even amid a flurry of tactical initiatives, in our view Sears Holdings still does not clearly stand for anything so compelling that consumers make Sears (or Kmart) their destination of choice. And perhaps that was never Lampert's true intention; the press and some industry pundits conjectured that Mr. Lampert's financial expertise was being used to create larger profits as opposed to creating real retail value.

Is There a Sears in Our Future?

Today there are many focused "masters" competing in each of Sears' many businesses. Indeed, Sears' thirty-year quest to regain its former glory has certainly eroded its relevance to consumers, or at least severely tested their patience.

Simply put, Sears is still in the middle of a perfect storm. The seminal question is whether the following three storm fronts will allow Sears the time to find their position:

1. **Consumers:** Today they have unlimited equal or better shopping choices, and their attitudes, behavior and demographics have changed in favor of Sears' competitors, many of whom are located closer to where the consumers live. This raises the attendant issue of Sears' captivity in malls and how it will deal with this issue. The challenge for Sears is to create experiences for the consumer and build a strong emotional connection that propels them into the stores— even if that's a little farther than the consumer would normally go.

2. **Competitors:** Sears must focus on competitors who have more efficient and effective business models, positioned with dominant value promises and elevated shopping experiences, attacking each or several of the conglomeration of Sears' arguably waning businesses (appliances and tools included). This includes a repositioned JCPenney, as well as competitors such as Wal-Mart, Kohl's, Target, Home Depot, Lowe's and the multiplicity of specialty chains, all of which have a major advantage because of their lower operating costs and real estate flexibility. Thus they gain more pricing leverage and greater profitability, as well as better proximity to the consumer.

Between 1998 and 2010, the number of competitors within a fifteen-minute drive from Sears grew from 1,400 to 4,300 stores, according to an analysis conducted by Kurt Salmon Associates using Claritas Data 2009.[9] Furthermore, during this period, Sears has failed to develop a preemptive e-commerce strategy and lags in the application of other leading-edge distribution platforms (e.g., mobile technology).

3.   **Economy and Industry Dynamics:** A weakened, postrecession economy, an oversaturated retail industry and the overall down-trending of the channel that Sears competes in all provide very little wiggle room and no more time for drifting.

We believe there can be a Sears in our future. But it will have to revisit its roots and the strategic drivers that made it the paragon of retailing throughout the world. It must reposition its model, based on the three strategic operating principles we can't get enough of: a neurologically compelling shopping experience; preemptive, precise and perpetual distribution; and total control of the value chain, without which the first two are impossible. The question is, does Sears have enough time and capital to execute this change? Or will the clock run out first?

CONCLUSION

MODELS FOR THE FUTURE

The marketplace has arrived at Wave III after a roller coaster ride of strategic and structural shifts over the last century. The unparalleled growth of the U.S. economy during that time has resulted in market saturation, despite exponential consumption growth due to the widespread availability of an unprecedented selection of goods and services. In essence, consumers today have thousands of equally compelling stores, websites, products, brands and services—right at their fingertips. They have the power of total accessibility.

Consumers have faster and cheaper access to more products due to globalization, technology and increased productivity. They utilize rapid, responsive, and the multitude of new-distribution platforms (e-commerce, kiosks, in-flight shopping, in-home events, etc.), and communicate information freely and easily on the Internet and mobile electronic devices.

Mobile access in particular is a twenty-first century game-changer, making that old retail real estate adage for success— "location, location, location"—a non-starter. Simply identifying the center of town or a space in the mall as a high-traffic area doesn't cut it today. The location must now be "mobile," both physically and electronically, to even have a chance. And, in the greatest challenge of all, retailers, brands, products or services can no longer just approach their customers. Today, companies must be invited or otherwise permitted into customers' lives.

And if a retailer or brand is permitted into the consumer's space, or if the consumer chooses to go to a particular store, website, or TV channel, the experience must be overwhelmingly compelling, or the company risks never getting the consumer back. In fact, we posit that the experience must be neurologically "addictive" for a business to achieve optimal success. In chapter 5, we referred to research findings of the human brain releasing a dopamine rush at the very mention of a brand such as Apple, Starbucks or Abercrombie & Fitch, so strong it compels consumers to rush back to those brands without even considering competitive options.

Over-abundance of choice enables consumers to demand more, which in turn drives competitors to perpetually innovate with new products, services and features around the shopping experience. So even having compelling "stuff," however new, on its own is also a non-starter. Retailing *must* also be a neurologically stimulating experience.

All of this is meant to underscore that, in the current environment—which we have defined as retailing's "Third Wave"—retailers, wholesalers, brands and services must completely transform their business strategies and models to survive.

A good framework for this transformation would be based on the five major shifts in consumer desires that have occurred in recent years. These are the dynamics that retailers and all consumer-facing industries must understand, respond to and deliver. These shifts are:

- **From needing stuff to demanding experiences:** The experience of A&F's "sexy" night club atmosphere trumps buying a pair of jeans off of a department store shelf.

- **From conformity to customization:** Today, ubiquitous brands like Levi's and Gap are struggling; niche brands are in.
- **From plutocracy to democracy:** Consumers want accessible luxury: Norma Kamali at Wal-mart; Mossimo, Cynthia Rowley and others at Target; Vera Wang at Kohl's; Nicole Miller at JC Penney, etc.
- **From wanting new to demanding new *and* demanding it now:** What's new today is cloned tomorrow: "fast fashion" of Zara, H&M, Forever 21, etc., which seem to produce two new lines every week.
- **From self to community:** Community and environmental initiatives employed by businesses are no longer marketing or PR projects. They are trends that will win consumers.

The Three Imperative Strategic Operating Principles for Success

To respond to and satisfy these consumer demands—and thus survive and grow—businesses must excel in all value chain functions, including marketing and innovation, just to achieve competitive parity. However, they must achieve *superiority* in the following strategic operating principles:

Neurological Connectivity

Today, as consumers expect the moon and stars—because they can—the retailer or brand must far exceed their expectations. They must co-create (with the customer) an experience that indelibly connects with their mind. It must be a holistic experience, consisting of pre-shopping anticipation, shopping ecstasy, and consumption satisfaction, and it must be so emotionally compelling that the customer wants to repeat it upon the mere mention of the brand or retailer's name. Even when established, however, it is not static, and requires constant reinforcing, often with subtle changes. But executed correctly, the brand-consumer connection preempts competition.

Preemptive Distribution

This is the necessity to gain access to consumers in front of the multiplicity of equally compelling products or services—by existing precisely where, when and how the consumer wants you. Preemptive distribution relies on speed, agility and the ability to reinforce the neurological connection, or brand promise. By definition, this requires an integrated matrix of all possible distribution mediums, including distribution into faster growing international markets.

Value Chain Control

No consumer-facing business can achieve the highest levels of a neurological connection and preemptive distribution without complete control of their value chain, from creation all the way to consumption. This control is especially important in those parts of the chain that touch and connect with the consumer: namely, market research, where knowledge about the consumer and their dreams is determined; production and marketing, where the "dream" experience is created; and finally, the point-of-sale, where the experience must be competently delivered. This defines a vertically integrated (though not necessarily owned), controlled business model.

The retailers and wholesalers who understand how these strategies ultimately satisfy and win consumers are transforming their business models right now. Some of the steps they are taking include:

Value Chain Integration

- Retailers integrating "backward" (accelerated pursuit of private and/or exclusive brands)
- Wholesalers integrating "forward" (opening their own branded retail chains)

Structural Realignment

- Segmentation (to compete in an infinite number of finite market niches)
- Consolidation (to leverage "back-end" supply chain for scale and productivity synergies)

Multi-distribution Formats

- Smaller stores as "neighborhood" extensions
- E-commerce sites
- Social networks (including transactional platforms)
- Mobile devices (smart phones, for example)
- In-flight shopping services
- TV
- "Pop-up" stores
- Catalogs, kiosks, in-home, door-to-door and others
- Non-traditional platforms of opportunity (ball parks, museums, etc.)

Market Expansion

- Niche branding by specialty chain brands
- Brand proliferation—accelerated line/style cycles
- Growing globally

New Names for New Models

Our thesis predicts that the traditional definitions of "retail" and "wholesale" will be irrelevant in the future because only those who transform their business models based on our three strategic operating principles will survive in the future. Therefore, for those that do, they will simply be perceived by consumers as brands. The retail or wholesale distinction will no longer be meaningful to consumers. Distinct brand names will provide the only worthwhile definition of value, whether it's the nameplates of stores or the labels on the products in the store. The new business models for retailer and wholesalers alike will be those that can best implement the three imperative strategic operating principles defined earlier.

The following are the strategic and structural highlights of the transformed traditional retail and wholesale models as covered in depth in chapter 8 under the sub-head: "Collapse Through Conversion."

Essentially, transformed retailers and wholesalers, now defined as brands, will render value chains seamless, with value controlled, managed and distributed by its creator all the way from creation to consumption.

In cases where it is absolutely necessary to collaborate with a second party at some point in the value chain, we predict that the creator will still manage and control their value within the second-party's sphere. Bloomingdale's, for example, in the midst of transforming their business model, would grow their own private brands as well as demanding brand exclusivity from outside branded vendors—the combination of these two facets eventually making up 80 to 90 percent of the merchandise they sell. We believe they will also lease the remaining space (or make some other financial-sharing arrangement) to designers such as Ralph Lauren or globally powerful brands such as The North Face, who will manage and control their brands in the "hosted" Blooming-dale's space.

Likewise, we predict that 80 to 90 percent of strong brands' revenues will come from their own retail outlets. And traditional wholesale brands, such as Warnaco's Olga Intimates, may join with a branded apparel specialty retailer such as Talbot's. Both target identical consumers: Warnaco would benefit from Talbot's retailing skills, and Talbot's would gain another product category and strong existing brand—a win-win.

Finally, retailers such as JC Penney, Macy's and others will lease space to other strong retail brands, as is already the case with Sephora and Mango in JCPenney and Sun Glass Hut and Mother-hood Maternity in Macy's. Perhaps soon, other department stores will follow suit by inviting Victoria's Secret, Soma and others into their historically share-losing "intimates" space. Not only would they gain the synergy of two go-to brands; they'd also increase space productivity. And, of course, the branded retail "renters" would get immediate preemptive distribution (department store locations everywhere), for low capital investment.

All new business entities will be strategically conceived to provide maximum access to consumers, and positioned to gain maximum access for the business. Therefore, they will operate in a multitude of distribution channels (clicks, bricks and catalogs), with a multitude of different formats (from small, convenient, and flexible to larger, all-inclusive destinations), and all will compete in as many consumer, product and retail sectors as the brand or service entity can credibly pursue. Also, the "back end" functions—operations, production, logistics and distribution—will be tightly centralized for maximum scale leverage and productivity synergies, as well as to support the enormously complex and segmented front ends of their businesses.

Incidentally, this redefinition of retail favors the current apparel specialty chain model over others, due to the fact that the store is the brand and the brand is the store, and that most of them already do control their supply chains. Therefore, they are best positioned among all sectors for preemptive distribution and the delivery of a neurologically connecting experience.

Finally, we predict that e-retailing, including mobile commerce and TV retailing, will continue to grow. However, we also believe that players who currently operate exclusively in this space (such as Amazon and eBay) will eventually open brick-and-mortar stores for the purposes of preemptive distribution, as well as enhanced delivery of the neurological experience.

The below highlights of the transformed traditional models encapsulate all the foregoing and essentially represent the "new rules" for successful change and the effective implementation of our three strategic operating principles.

Rules for Transforming Traditional Retailers

Change the Retail Value Proposition
Become a branded neurological experience, not a store

Adopt a New Structure
Reorganize around lifestyles

Accelerate Private and Exclusive Branding and/or
Lease Space to Compatible Brands
Cede control to brands

Results
Synergy-creating organic growth

Preemptively Access Consumers with:
- Larger urban "lifestyle experiential emporiums"
- Smaller free-standing neighborhood stores
- Private branded specialty chains (e.g., INC and Arizona Stores)

- New channels of opportunity (Pop-ups, In Home, etc.)
- Integration of all distribution platforms (Clicks/Bricks/ Catalogs)

Rules for Transforming Traditional Wholesalers

Change the Wholesale Value Proposition

Become a portfolio of lifestyle-branded retail specialty chains providing neurologically connecting experiences

Adopt a New Structure

Reorganize around preemptive distribution strategies through all possible platforms and mediums ("clicks, bricks, catalogs" and more), including

- Providing exclusive brands to transformed retailers
- Selecting compatible transformed retailers to lease space for total management and control of individual brands
- Pursue co-branding joint ventures with compatible retail specialty chain brands

Results
Synergy-creating fundamental new growth

New Rule for Evolving Branded Retail Specialty Chains

Given the fact that this sector is best strategically positioned for maximum and successful implementation of our three strategic operating principles, some of its more successful brands as listed in earlier chapters led the evolution to preemptively sub-branding into multiple product and consumer market niches (such as J. Crew sub-branding Crewcuts for kids, Madewell for "boomers" and J.Crew Bridal; Abercrombie & Fitch to abercrombie for tweens and Hollister for teens; and many others). Much of the impetus for this new direction emanated from both consumers' demand for more special, lesser known brands and the lesson learned from the Gap's attempt to spread its brand across all consumer segments, which required a huge investment in expansion but is now greatly challenged.

New Rule for E-and-M-Commerce "Pure-Play" Brands

This newest and fastest growing retail sector, (such as Amazon, Zappos, eBay, Gilt Groupe, social networks, as well as the older QVC and HSN), must also transform its models to embody our three operating principles. As suggested throughout the book, the most successful brands, such as those mentioned above, are all striving to create great experiences as opposed to simply providing convenience. And, as Zappos exemplified early on, controlling the value chain of their brands is paramount to delivering those experiences. The newest rule for this sector will be driven by its need for greater preemptive distribution. As pointed out in chapter 6, we believe this will ultimately lead to e-commerce expanding its distribution to include brick and mortar stores, within which they can better provide the neurological experience, particularly for those products requiring a more "touchy-feely" experience such as apparel.

Back to the Future? Not Really

Many experts and colleagues of ours today, as well as you, our reader, could argue that the department stores of Wave I ("palaces of consumption"), and even the Sears catalog and, later in that wave, its early mall dominance, were all operating on our three strategic principles, although unarticulated. And we would agree to a limited extent.

They were providing an enjoyable shopping experience, although not to the level of neurologically addictive. Their distribution was as good as could be expected, given the economic and distribution infrastructure of the United States at the time, as well as the lack of globalization and technology advancements. Therefore, the term preemptive distribution did not exist, because the reality of it couldn't. Finally, total control of one's value chain was an impossibility without the enablers of technology and globalization.

Wave II was like a harmonic convergence of equal parts economic growth, consumer demand, infrastructure building, marketing and advertising, innovation, mobility and geographic expansion, and the leading edges of new technology and globalization.

Then the seemingly equal parts of the convergence, which were all harmoniously driving unprecedented prosperity for all, became unequal. Abundance grew to overabundance, which provided consumers with unlimited selection and thus the power to demand more from suppliers. This imbalance of overcapacity chasing slower population and demand growth set the stage for Wave III, and the necessity for businesses to transform their models around our operating principles merely to survive.

However, neither our new rules nor their transformation would have been possible without major advancements in technology, including the Internet and globalization.

Wave III finds consumers in the center of the universe, with all parts focused on pleasing them—period. Furthermore, while consumers may go to stores or tap into sites or order from a catalog, the word "retail" is meaningless to them. And while they may buy wholesale brands, they do not know or care where the brand was made or by whom. Therefore, those who do survive and succeed, transforming their models to our new rules, will neither be, nor should they call themselves, retailers or wholesalers. Because in the minds of the consumers, which are the only minds that count in Wave III, they will all simply be brands.

So at the end of the day (and our book), those that succeed will be brand managers with the sole responsibility of managing and controlling the preemptive distribution of their neurologically addictive brand from its creation all the way through to consumption.

NOTES

Prologue

1. Christina C. Berk, "J. Crew CEO: Retailers Have Come Back, Not Consumers." CNBC, http://www.cnbc.com/id/36273496/J_Crew_CEO_Retailers_Have_Come_Back_Not_Consumers.
2. Meeting attended by author, October 29, 2008.
3. David Moin, "The Big Fix: Allen I. Questrom's Recipe for Survival in Turbulent Times," *Women's Wear Daily*, November 12, 2008: 4.
4. Lee Scott, Keynote Speech at the National Retail Federation's 2009 Annual Convention, New York City, January 12, 2009.
5. Sharon Edelson, "Shopping Is So Passé: Wal-Mart CEO Foresees New Consumer Mind-Set," *Women's Wear Daily*, January 13, 2009: 1.

Introduction

1. Personal conversation with the author, *Women's Wear Daily* Summit Meeting, 2006.
2. Ira Neimark, *Crossing Fifth Avenue to Bergdorf Goodman: An Insider's Account on the Rise of Luxury Retail* (New York: SPI Books, 2006).
3. Suzanne Kapner, "How Best Buy Plans to Beat Wal-Mart," *Fortune*, December 1, 2009, http://money.cnn.com/2009/11/30/technology/best_buy_wal_mart.fortune/index.htm.
4. "Wal-Mart Stores, Inc. F4Q10 Earnings Call Transcript," February 18, 2010, http://seekingalpha.com/article/189329-wal-mart-stores-inc-f4q10-qtr-end—01–31–10-earnings-call-transcript.
5. Brian Stelter, "Up Next: Reruns From HSN," *New York Times,* June 14, 2010, http://query.nytimes.com/gst/fullpage.html?res=9C05E4DD153DF937A25755C0A9669D8B63.
6. David Moin and Vicki M. Young, "Fleming: Amazon Stores a Threat to Wal-Mart," *Women's Wear Daily*, December 3, 2009, http://www.wwd.com/business-news/fleming-amazon-stores-a-threat-to-wal-mart–2384435.

Chapter 3

1. Venkatesan Vembu, "Transforming Giants," *DNA*, February 3, 2007, http://www.dnaindia.com/lifestyle/special_transforming-giants_1077797.

2. International Council of Shopping Centers data, 2010, http://www.icsc.org/srch/faq_category.php?cat_type=research&cat_id=3.
3. Peter Lyman and Hal R. Varian, "How Much Information," 2003, http://www.sims.berkeley.edu/how-much-info–2003.

Chapter 4

1. Abraham Maslow, "A Theory of Human Motivation," *Psychological Review* 50 (1943): 370–96. (The hierarchy of needs includes, in order: Physiological, Safety, Love/Belonging, Esteem, and Self-actualization.)
2. U.S. Census Bureau, Historical Income Tables, http://www.census.gov/hhes/www/income/data/historical/index.html.
3. Richard Easterlin, "Will Raising the Incomes of All Increase the Happiness of All?" *Journal of Economic Behavior and Organization* (1995): 35–47.
4. E. Diener and R. Biswas-Diener, "Will Money Increase Subjective Well-being? A Literature Review and Guide to Needed Research," *Social Indicators Research* 57 (2002): 119–69
5. Daniel Kahneman, "Would You Be Happier If You Were Richer? A Focusing Illusion," Princeton University, CEPS Working Paper No. 125, May 2006.
6. Travis Carter and Thomas Gilovich, "The Relative Relativity of Material and Experiential Purchases," *Journal of Personality and Social Psychology*, Cornell University, 2010.
7. Barry Schwartz, *The Paradox of Choice: Why More Is Less*, New York: Ecco, 2004.
8. Unpublished interview with the author.
9. David Moin, "Bloomingdale's Opens Store in Dubai," *Women's Wear Daily*, February 1, 2010.
10. Ben Fischman, "Retailers Can Transform Operations by Creatively Integrating New Technology: A Wharton School Conference Explores the Reality of Retailing in a Web 2.0 World," lecture, Macy's Herald Square, New York, March 23, 2010.
11. Personal conversation with the author.
12. Pia Sarkar, "Stores Boost Sales with Own Labels / National Brands Face Increasing Competition," *SFGate.com,* May 5, 2006. http://articles.sfgate.com/2006–05–05/business/17294456_1_wal-mart-private-brands-private-label.
13. PLMA Consumer Research Report. http://www.plma.com/PLMA_Store_Brands_and_the_Recession.pdf.
14. Kevin Lindsay, "How to Make Online Shopping Feel Like 'Real' Shopping," *Apparel*, September 10, 2008, http://www.apparelmag.com/ME2/dirmod.asp?sid=&nm=&type=news&mod=News&mid=9A02E3B96F2A415ABC72CB5F516B4C10&tier=3&nid=04556E590A40483F8B8ADB73F8C1D6A0.
15. Tara Parker-Pope, "This Is Your Brain at the Mall: Why Shopping Makes You Feel Good," *Wall Street Journal*, December 6, 2005.
16. Emily Steel, "Nestlé Takes a Beating on Social-Media Sites," *Wall Street Journal,* March 29, 2010, http://online.wsj.com/article/SB10001424052702304434404575149883850508158.html?mod=rss_media_marketing.

Chapter 5

1. Kasra Ferdows, Michael A. Lewis and Jose A. D. Machuca, "Rapid Fire Fulfillment," *Harvard Business Review* 82 (2004): 104–10.
2. John Luciew, "Hershey Learns at Retail Stores How to Get Its Candy into Your Head," *Associated Press,* February 16, 2010.
3. Ilan Brat, "The Emotional Quotient of Soup Shopping," *Wall Street Journal,* February 17, 2010, http://online.wsj.com/article/SB1000142405274870480 4204575069562743700340.html.
4. Eric R. Kandel, James H. Schwartz and Thomas M. Jessel, eds., *Principles of Neural Science, 4th ed,* (New York: McGraw-Hill, 2000).
5. C. K. Prahalad and Venkatram Ramaswamy, "The New Frontier of Experience Innovation," *MIT Sloan Management Review Summer* 44:4 (2003), http://socialmediaclub.pbworks.com/f/cocreation.pdf.
6. Robert Epstein, "How Science Can Help You Fall in Love," *Scientific American,* January 2010.
7. Ximena Arriaga & Christopher Agnew, "Being Committed: Affective, Cognitive, and Conative Components of Relationship Commitment," *Personality and Social Psychology Bulletin* 27 (2001): 1190–1203.
8. Ivor Morgan and Jay Rao, "Making Routine Customer Experiences Fun," *MIT Sloan Management Review,* October 15, 2003.
9. Army Experience Center, http://www.thearmyexperience.com/.
10. Manasee Wagh, "Peace Group Protests Army Center at Mall," *The Intelligencer,* November 29, 2009, http://www.phillyburbs.com/news/news_details/article/27/2009/november/28/peace-group-protests-army-center-at-mall.html.

Chapter 6

1. Robert A. Iger, "A Message in Every Medium" (Keynote Interview, *Financial Times* Business of Luxury Summit, Los Angeles, CA, June 13–15 2010).
2. Sandra M. Jones, "U.S. Retailers Venture Overseas for Growth," *Chicago Tribune,* July 6, 2010, http://www.chicagotribune.com/business/ct-biz-0706-global-retail-20100706,0,3805667.story.
3. David Moin, "Gap Launching China Strategy," *Women's Wear Daily,* June 24, 2010.

Chapter 7

1. Personal conversation with the author, *Women's Wear Daily* Summit Meeting, 2006.
2. Personal conversation with the author.
3. *MIT Sloan Management Review,* Winter 2010. p. 19.
4. Liana B. Baker, "On the Hunt for the Next Bay Area Delicacy," *Wall Street Journal,* June 3, 2010.
5. KSA Study, 2007.

Chapter 8

1. The source for the above statistics is *NPD (National Panel Data),* a consumer panel tracking and research company.

2. Discussion with Robin Lewis, early April 2010.
3. Press Release, *Procter & Gamble,* May 25, 2010, http://www.marketwire. com/press-release/Tide-Dry-Cleaners-Is-Changing-Dry-Cleaning-Business-Good-Seeking-Local-Entrepreneurs-NYSE-PG–1265979.htm.
4. Susan Reda, "With SKU Reductions Underway, Which Will Survive?" *Stores,* February 2010.
5. Ibid.
6. *CIA World Factbook,* https://www.cia.gov/library/publications/the-world-factbook/geos/ch.html; Globalis, http://globalis.gvu.unu.edu/indicator_ detail.cfm?IndicatorID=19&Country=CN.
7. Chery Automobile Co., Ltd. was founded in 1997 by five of Anhui's local state owned investment companies with an initial capitalization of RMB 3.2 billion. Plant construction commenced on March 18, 1997 in Wuhu, Anhui Province, China. The first car came off the production line on December 18, 1999. Ports 1961 was founded in 1961 by the late Luke Tanabe.
8. Kathy Chen, "U.S. Cities Seek to Woo Chinese Investment," *Wall Street Journal,* April 6, 2010. http://online.wsj.com/article/SB10001424052702303410 404575151593460208482.html.
9. "New Masters of Management," *Economist,* April 17, 2010.
10. Dennis K. Berman, "Lazard's Statesman, a Game-Changer," *Wall Street Journal,* April 13, 2010, http://online.wsj.com/article/SB100014240527023045 06904575180363245274300.html?ru=MKTW&mod=MKTW.
11. Jonathan Birchall, "Criticism That Spread Like a Rash," *Financial Times,* May 26, 2010.
12. Melanie Wells, "Kid Nabbing," *Forbes,* February 2, 2004, http://www.forbes. com/forbes/2004/0202/084.html.
13. Tim Bradshaw and David Gelles, "Facebook Targets China and Russia," *Financial Times,* June 23, 2010. http://www.ft.com/cms/s/2/35b709ae–7ec4–11df-ac9b–00144feabdc0.html.

Chapter 10

1. Phone conversation with author.
2. Personal conversation with the author, *Women's Wear Daily* Summit Meeting, 2006.
3. "Our Strategy," VF Corporation website, http://www.vfc.com/about/our-strategy.
4. "Growth Drivers," VF Corporation website, http://www.vfc.com/about/our-strategy/growth-drivers.
5. Joshua Freed, "Best Buy Overhauling Stores to Hit Segments," Associated Press, May 19, 2004.
6. Suzanne Kapner, "How Best Buy Plans to beat Wal-Mart," *Fortune.com,* December 1, 2009, http://money.cnn.com/2009/11/30/technology/best_buy_ wal_mart.fortune/index.htm.
7. Personal conversation between the author and Alexis Maybank, May 2010
8. Ibid.
9. Ibid.
10. HSN Interactive, http://www.hsni.com/.

11. Brian Stetler, "Up Next: Reruns From HSN," *New York Times,* June 14, 2010, http://query.nytimes.com/gst/fullpage.html?res=9C05E4DD153DF937A25 755C0A9669D8B63.

12. "Key Retailer Interview with Mindy Grossman, CEO, HSN, Inc.," World Retail Congress 2010, http://www.worldretailcongress.com/page.cfm/link=316.

13. Linda Moss, "Samsung will launch HSN Shop by Remote App on its Internet@TV—Connect Service," Homeshoppingista, January 8, 2010, http://homeshoppingista.wordpress.com/category/corporate-information/comcast-corporate-information/.

14. Personal conversation with the author.

15. Mark Veverka, "The World's Best Retailer," *Barron's,* March 30, 2009, http://online.barrons.com/article/SB123819715466061661.html.

16. Amazon Q3 2009 Earnings Call Transcript, http://seekingalpha.com/article/168333-amazon-q3–2009-earnings-call-transcript?part=qanda.

17. AMZN 2009 10-K filing, pg. 27.

18. Amazon Fresh, https://fresh.amazon.com.

19. Tony Hsieh, "How I Did It: Tony Hsieh, CEO, Zappos.com," as told to Max Chafkin, *Inc.,* September 1, 2006, http://www.inc.com/magazine/20060901/hidi-hsieh.html.

20. Tony Hsieh, "Tony Hsieh: Redefining Zappos' Business Model," as told to Diane Brady, *Bloomberg BusinessWeek,* May 27, 2010, http://www.businessweek.com/magazine/content/10_23/b4181088591033.htm.

21. "Zappos Family Core Values," http://about.zappos.com/our-unique-culture/zappos-core-values.

22. Tony Hsieh, "CEO Letter," July 22, 2009, http://blogs.zappos.com/ceoletter.

23. "Apple Inc. F4Q09 Earnings Call Transcript," October 19, 2009, http://seekingalpha.com/article/167404-apple-f4q09-qtr-end–9–26–09-earnings-call-transcript.

Chapter 11

1. Heide B. Malhotra, "Gap's Social Responsibility Driving Retail Growth," *The Epoch Times,* May 3, 2010. http://www.theepochtimes.com/n2/content/view/34620/.

2. Patricia Sellers, "Starbucks: The Next Generation," *Fortune,* April 4, 2005, http://money.cnn.com/magazines/fortune/fortune_archive/2005/04/04/8255923/index.htm.

3. Howard Schultz, "Text of Starbucks Memo," February 14, 2007, http://online.wsj.com/public/article/SB117234084129218452-hpbDoP_cLbOUdc G_0y7qLlQ7Okg_20080224.html?mod=rss_free

4. "The Proof is in the Cup: Starbucks Launches Historic New Pike Place Roast ™," Starbucks Newsroom, April 7, 2008, http://news.starbucks.com/article_display.cfm?article_id=51.

5. "Financial Release," March 19, 2008, http://investor.starbucks.com/phoenix.zhtml?c=99518&p=irol-newsArticle&ID=1120352&highlight=.

6. "Starbucks Will Close 900 More Stores," *Retailer Daily,* April 2, 2009, http://www.retailerdaily.com/entry/12841/starbucks-will-close–900-more-stores/.

7. Ibid.

8. Sarah Gilbert, "Dunkin' Donuts beats Starbucks with better tasting coffee . . . again," BloggingStocks, October 20, 2008. http://www.blogging stocks.com/2008/10/20/dunkin-donuts-beats-starbucks-with-better-tasting-coffee-aga/.

Chapter 12

1. Donald R. Katz, *The Big Store: Inside the Crisis and Revolution at Sears* (New York: Viking Press, 1987).
2. Ibid.
3. Rosabeth Moss Kanter, *On the Frontiers of Management,* (Cambridge, MA: Harvard Business Press, 2003).
4. Robin Lewis, "Strategic Insight in to the Decline of a Great American Icon," *Robin Reports,* January 2003—April 2003.
5. Ibid.
6. Ibid.
7. Arthur C. Martinez, *The Hard Road to the Softer Side: Lessons from the Transformation of Sears,* (New York: Crown Business, 2001).
8. Personal interview with the author.
9. Lewis.

INDEX